Fine Art
Photoshop

Lessons in Digital Drawing and Painting

**Michael J. Nolan
and Renée LeWinter**

with

Tim Amrhein, Nathan Clement, and Barbara Kordesh

Hayden
Books

Fine Art Photoshop

Library of Congress Catalog Number: 97-81026
ISBN: 1-56205-829-0

Copyright © 1998 Hayden Books

Printed in the United States of America 1 2 3 4 5 6 7 8 9 0

This book was produced digitally by Macmillan Computer Publishing and manufactured using computer-to-plate technology (a film-less process) by GAC/Shepard Poorman, Indianapolis, Indiana.

Warning and Disclaimer

Trademark Acknowledgments

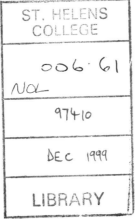

Publisher	Jordan Gold
Executive Editor	Beth Millett
Managing Editor	Brice Gosnell
Acquisitions Editor	John Kane
Development Editor	Linda Laflamme
Technical Editor	Gary Kubicek
Project Editor	Kevin Laseau
Copy Editors	Michael Brumitt San Dee Philips
Cover Designer	Ruth Harvey
Book Designer	Renée LeWinter
Production Team	Marcia Deboy Michael Dietsch Cynthia Fields Maureen West
Indexer	Ben Slen

About the Authors

Michael J. Nolan practices "design for the information age" working with clients and collaborators, editors and output houses, artists and art directors, packagers and marketing managers from coast to coast on design projects ranging from corporate identities to books and web sites for his company, N•fo. He is the co-founder of one of the country's first digital studios, PRINTZ Electronic Design in San Francisco. He freely admits being "dazzled by pixels" and paints with Photoshop every chance he gets. The author of *PageMaker® 5 Expert Techniques*, Michael writes on design issues as a contributor to *WebWeek Magazine*.

Renée LeWinter is an artist, print/multimedia designer, and computer imaging consultant based in Somerville, Massachusetts. She is the coauthor of *Photoshop Web Magic* and *Web Animation for Dummies*. Her articles have appeared in publications such as *Computer Graphics World* (for which she was a contributing editor), *Computer Artist*, *U&lc*, *Siggraph Daily*, and *Electronic Publishing*. As the former head of an undergraduate visual and media design program in Boston, Renée developed extensive curriculum to introduce design and computer graphics concepts to artists, designers, and business professionals.

Renée's paintings and prints have been exhibited nationally and internationally. She was an artist-in-residence at The School of Visual Arts, Master of Fine Arts program in Computer Art, and her paintings were featured in Pixel and Computer Artist magazines. On-line, Renée's paintings can be seen at the 911 Gallery Web site: *http://www.911gallery.org/911*.

Dedication

To Eileen and Jackson with love—Michael

For Adam, Zachary, Lilly and Dylan—Renée

Acknowledgments

We would like to take this opportunity to thank Mary Ann Kearns, Director, 911 Gallery (*http://www.911gallery.org/911*) for graciously agreeing to write our Foreword.

CalComp, Input Technologies Division, Scottsdale, AZ (*http://www.calcomp.com/*) for the loan of the UltraSlate tablets.

Carol Reid, Director of Marketing, Digital Stock Corporation (*http://www.digitalstock.com*) for permission to use photographs from theDigital Stock collection.

Flo Scott, Electronic Imaging Center, Boston, MA, for the use of her photograph.

Steve Boulter, Vice President, Parrot Digigraphics, Inc, Burlington, MA for providing contact information and advice regarding trends in fine-art digital printmaking.

Janet Wardlaw for the loan of her cabin, pond, and boat in sweet Owen County, Indiana.

Tom McMillan, Editor of Electronic Publishing, for permission to reuse excerpts from the "Fine Art Goes to IRIS" article.

Henry Wilhelm, Wilhelm Imaging Research, Inc., Grinnell, IA, for permission to reproduce his ink and media test results.

Mac Holbert, cofounder and operations manager for Nash Editions, Manhattan Beach, CA, for his commentary about fine-art digital printmaking.

Jon Cone, Cone Editions, East Topsham, VT for his continued advice and suggestions about fine-art digital printmaking.

David and Sherry Rogelberg, and Brian Gill, our agents at Studio B, for their continued support and friendship.

Acquisitions Editor John Kane, Technical Editor Gary Kubicek, Development Editor Linda Laflamme, Project Editor Dayna Isley, Executive Editor Beth Millett, and Project Editor Kevin Laseau for their consummate professionalism.

Special thanks to Barbara Kordesh, Nathan Clement and Tim Amrhein.

Hayden Books

The staff of Hayden Books is committed to bringing you the best computer books. What our readers think of Hayden is important to our ability to serve our customers. If you have any comments, no matter how great or how small, we'd appreciate your taking the time to send us a note.

You can reach Hayden Books at the following:

Hayden Books
201 West 103rd Street
Indianapolis, IN 46290
317-581-3833

Visit the Macmillan Web site at *http://www.mcp.com.*

Contents at a glance:

Part I: Drawing and Sketching

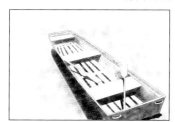

This lesson covers the picture plane, perspective, point of view, dot, line, value, texture, freehand drawing, and the crosshatch technique.

Draw a self portrait and learn about the shape of the head, position of facial features, lighting, expression, compositional placement, line and pattern, and surface texture.

Study the figure-ground relationship, the additive process, receding space, silhouette, grouping, volume, shape, value and texture as you use the Airbrush.

Learn measurement, proportion, the effects of light and shadow on architectural surfaces.

Part II: The Digital Palette

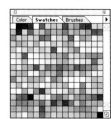

Atmosphere, light, emotion, color combinations, adjacent and complementary colors, expression, hue, and value are the subjects of this lesson.

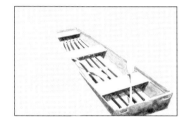

Use transparency, blending, and learn about tonality, light, shadow, contrast and value as you paint the boat in a watercolor style in this lesson.

Study the color palettes of different races and ethnic groups, and color your self-portrait.

Hue, saturation, warm and cool colors, simultaneous contrast, depth of field and volume are some of the concepts covered in this lesson.

Part III: Enhancing Your Technique and Style

Use broad brushes to paint the water in the pond as you learn about negative shape and color balance.

Realism, abstract expressionism, the additive process, and the painting surface are some of the subjects of this lesson.

Adding elements to a painting to make it tell a story is covered in this lesson, as well as concepts of volume, light, reflectivity, balance and contrast.

Learn to create realistic architectural textures such as wood, metal and glass in this lesson.

Part IV: More Special Effects

Foreword Pigment to pixel

By Mary Ann Kearns,
Director, 911 Gallery
http://www.911gallery.org/911

Digital art has at last arrived! With high-caliber digital prints finally embraced by collectors and museums, today's digital artist is free of the toilsome task of arguing the merits and credibility of the medium.

The digital artist can now concentrate on the challenge at hand: creating a unique visual experience embued with personal expression. Although advancements in computer tools have made digital imaging more intuitive than ever, the fundamental task remains the same. All fine art, including digital art, is a creative exploration conceived in the mind and skillfully realized with the hand and eye.

Visitors to 911 Gallery, which specializes in digital art, might not even realize that the art they see was created on a computer. High resolution prints on a variety of papers and materials are a far cry from the readily identified pixelated computer graphics of barely a decade ago. When a visitor exclaims, "This is all so new," I inform them that, in fact, computer art is not a recent development in the arts.

To put digital art in context, one must remember that artists began using computers as soon as they had access. As early as the mid-1960s, computer artists used cumbersome CAD programs to create images that they were lucky to print on X-Y pen plotters. These artists were most often by necessity programmers as well. Their art was generated in another realm—the realm of the "machine." When computer art was first practiced, the computer program was as much an art form as the completed image. Computer graphics typically involved blind input in the form of programming that was based on coordinates or algorithms. Code written by the artist therefore generated a range of geometric patterns and designs.

By the late 1970s, the personal computer was introduced. Although it had a tiny screen and limited palette, it represented a great advance and was readily adopted by artists. Combined with input from the video camera, computer art began to incorporate elements captured from real life and moved away from programming.

In the mid-1980s, software with graphic user interfaces arrived, as well as programs that simulated art toolboxes. Along with more sophisticated software came advances in hardware as well, including video cards capable of displaying millions of colors. The introduction of Photoshop in the late 1980s enabled artists to import photographs that could be retouched, composited, and manipulated. Equally important, Photoshop was also a "paint" program, a sophisticated emulation of traditional art media.

Using the computer and software to explore photographic manipulation is one avenue of expression available to artists today. Photoshop does infinitely more than eliminate the mess of paint or the odor of chemicals. More is made possible than just an impressive palette of colors. The use of this program changes the very nature of the creative act because the making of digital paintings is no longer confined to a linear process.

Among the myriad of tools in Photoshop, layering is arguably the richest, both literally and figuratively. Compositional elements can be imported from a variety of sources, such as scans of real objects, drawings, photographs of nature, and other digital images. Built upon one another like glazes of oil paint, layers represent a veritable depository of symbols and metaphors. As the artist incorporates various elements in this fashion, each becomes a springboard for further exploration. Additional manipulation of saturation or opacity, as well as the use of filters, enhances the artist's range of expression.

The accessibility and impressive capabilities of today's ink-jet printers add a new dimension of excitement to computer imaging. Not long ago, artists seeking high-caliber prints sent their digital files to a service bureau, then nervously anticipated the cost-intensive result. No longer dependent upon print houses, today's artist has regained control of the printed image.

The creative process also need not end when the image is ready to print. Digital images can be printed directly on a variety of substrates including canvas, vellum, or transparent film. Artists can even choose to work back into their prints with traditional media. Due to the availability with mixed-media, the image can be printed over, or even scanned, reworked on the computer, and printed again. With a digital image, the possibilities are endless. The image onscreen is but one step in an open-ended process of discovery and expression.

An art historian with her eye on the future, Mary Ann Kearns is interested not in reinterpreting art styles that have come and gone but rather in promoting the emerging art of the next century. In 1992 Kearns founded 911 Gallery, one of the first exclusively digital galleries in the country. When it went on-line in 1994, it was one of the first galleries on the World Wide Web. Published in such varied periodicals as The Washington Post, ARTnews, *and* Computer Artist, *911 Gallery has made a significant contribution to the awareness and appreciation of digital media in the fine arts.*

Presentations by Kearns have included: "Virtual Gallery on the World Wide Web," to the National Endowment for the Arts in Washington, DC, and "The Dada Not Data Highway," a position statement that accompanied the Nam June Paik exhibit "The Electronic Super Highway" at the Indianapolis Museum of Art in 1995.

In July 1997 Kearns was project coordinator for the "Digital Atelier" at the National Museum of American Art, Smithsonian Institution. The "Digital Atelier" inspired the general public and artists alike with exposure to the impressive realm of possibilities afforded by new imaging and print technologies. Among her current projects, Kearns is on the steering committee for the Boston Cyberarts Festival, which will debut in and around the Boston area in the spring of 1999.

She looks forward to future developments in the creation and appreciation of digital media art and to participating in the shaping of the evolving digital aesthetic.

Introduction

Just as utilitarian and industrial processes, such as welding and neon light, quickly found their way into the hands of visual artists, it is natural and inevitable that computer hardware and software would lead to art. Adobe Photoshop's introduction in 1989 gave the artist tools and techniques that had never before existed, along with unprecedented control, flexibility, and speed. We are only beginning to see the impact of these digital tools on fine art.

Fine Art Photoshop is not about scanning a photo, applying a quick filter, and calling the result art. Instead, our intention for this book is to help the digital artist reconnect with some of the traditional principles for making fine art. The book is designed to help you link the pictures in your mind with the right digital tools and techniques to bring them to life.

Art meets technology

Making fine art with Photoshop combines all the traditional elements of art with much of the power of technology. And of course, for everything that is gained, something is lost. It's wonderful to be able to undo misplaced paint strokes or work in several layers, but what happens to texture when paint is no longer physically laid down on canvas? And although it's liberating to have millions of colors and a limitless number of brushes available, it's very confining when all your paintings must be made on the same desktop. Regardless of the limitations, these new digital tools have opened up more avenues for artistic expression than anyone dreamed possible.

How to find inspiration

Of course it's a cliché to say that things to paint are all around us, but it's undeniable that everyday objects and situations provide unlimited opportunities for artistic expression. Study subjects and look for pleasant arrangements of things, unusual juxtapositions, interesting textures and lighting effects, or something that tells a story. Whether you want to paint a portrait or still life, a landscape or a figure, first create a mental image of how your painting might look, including colors, technique, and medium.

One of the paintings in this book (the boat on a pond) began with a photo taken with a single-use camera. Photographs are an important component of creating art with Photoshop because unlike a traditional easel, your computer usually can't be set up in such places as beside a pond. Having a photo for reference lets you return over and over to the scene you're painting.

Of course, a traditional pencil and sketchpad come in handy whenever you begin to study a subject. By sketching your picture freehand, you gain an opportunity to discover details and relationships that you might otherwise miss, and you add your personal point of view. Later on, you can scan sketches and photos, and import them into Photoshop, adding possibilities for mixing media.

How to use this book

Now that familiar artist's tools such as pencils and paintbrushes and erasers and rulers have morphed into their digital equivalents, it's a challenge to learn how to use them all over again. It's also fun. This book gives you a digital framework for applying traditional artistic elements and concepts. We hope that by reading it you'll learn as much about art as you will software.

Work your way through *Fine Art Photoshop* as you would a traditional art instruction book. Begin with the section on sketching and drawing, which contains four exercises: a landscape, a still life, a portrait, and an architectural illustration. Become familiar with the basic tools and techniques and gradually build your skill level through more complex and detailed exercises. As you progress through the sections on color, style and technique, and filters/special effects, build upon your earlier work and develop a mastery of Photoshop's painting power.

You can do all of the lessons in a section, such as Drawing and Sketching, before moving on to the next group of lessons, or you can follow one project through all four sections. It's up to you. Also, feel free to adapt our instructions to suit your own artistic goals: brush settings, colors, shapes, and placement on the canvas can be your personal choices, though we recommend that you familiarize yourself with the lessons in succeeding sections before changing our suggestions to be sure your work lends itself to the processes being taught.

As you use this book, refer often to Part V, "The Photoshop paintbox," to become more familiar with brush settings and the options available to you with each of the painting tools. This section also provides examples of different kinds of brush strokes to help guide your choice of settings as you complete the drawing and painting lessons.

Technical Limitations and Considerations

When you begin using Photoshop to create fine art, you'll quickly come to see some of the program's limitations. File sizes for large, high-resolution illustrations and paintings can quickly become unmanageable, and adding layers, channels, and masks only makes things worse. You may not have enough RAM or storage space for the files you want to create, or for filter effects you want to apply. The lessons in *Fine Art Photoshop* generally require at least 24 MB of RAM; in some cases more than that is needed.

Workarounds do exist to solve some of these problems. If you have a storage device such as an Iomega Zip or Syquest drive, you can use a blank disk as the secondary scratch disk. Insert the blank Zip or Syquest disk, choose File➡Preferences➡Plug-Ins & Scratch Disks, and select the blank disk as the Secondary Scratch Disk. (You'll have to quit Photoshop and then re-open the program to put this choice into effect.) Another option is to acquire a large capacity hard disk and make it the Secondary Scratch Disk.

In some cases, you can lower the memory requirements for Photoshop; refer to the Photoshop manual for further information about doing this. Avoid using virtual RAM because it consumes too much of your hard disk and is painfully slow.

You might need to merge layers to make a file small enough to enable a filter to work, or you can select smaller portions of the file to apply an effect on one part, and then on the others.

This book is written for users on both the Macintosh and Windows platforms; instructions are given for both.

Using a graphics tablet

All of the lessons in this book were designed to be done with a standard mouse. However, if you want to become a serious Photoshop artist, you'll probably want to consider buying a graphics tablet. There are several tablets on the market from which to choose; we highly recommend the Calcomp Ultra Slate. Its convenient size and level of sensitivity make it an ideal choice for creating digital fine art.

So take a deep breath and begin thinking about Photoshop in a new way. Imagine a project with no deadlines, no fear of typos, no nagging clients or fussy art directors. This is about getting in touch with your creativity and harnessing it to one of the most powerful artistic tools ever invented!

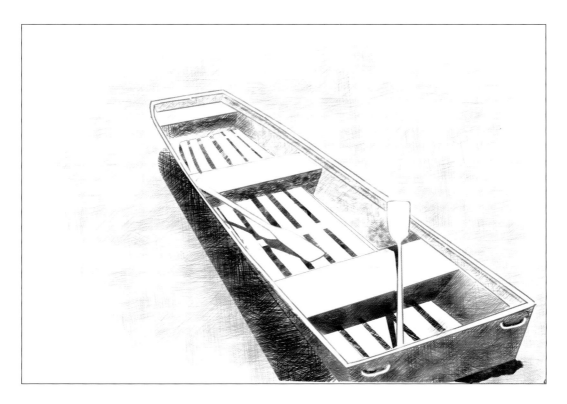

Part I: Lesson A Sketch a boat in "pencil"

Although it's certainly possible to scan a photograph into Photoshop and reduce it to an outline for your drawing or painting, doing so leaves out an essential art element: the artist's point of view. Any time you relinquish creative control to the software, your art becomes more programmed and less personal. Start from scratch, and the result will be unique.

For example, as you create a pencil sketch of a boat on a pond in this lesson, you make artistic decisions about the picture plane, dot and line,

Art concepts

Picture plane

Dot

Line

Point of view

Proportion

Grid

Perspective

Value

Texture

Freehand

Crosshatch

**Photoshop tools
and features**

Pencil tool

Pen tool

Paintbrush tool

Rubber Stamp tool

Line tool

Toning tools

Layers

Guides & Grid

point of view, proportion, grid, and perspective. The point of view in the photograph is from approximately 10 feet away, looking down on the subject. Notice how the front of the boat appears smaller than the back and how the lines defining the sides become closer to one another as they approach the front. If these lines were to continue past the front of the boat, they would eventually meet. This point of convergence is called the *vanishing point*.

It's not necessary to make a drawing just like the one here—in fact, make it your own interpretation as much as possible. *You* choose the point of view, crop the picture, and decide the proportions. Zoom in tighter, or imagine and create a larger scene.

This sketch serves as the basis for later lessons, during which you apply color, brush strokes, filtering, and other advanced techniques. When you finish the lesson, save two copies: a final pencil sketch and a work copy.

Figure I.A.1
Reference photograph shot using
a disposable camera.

Choose a drawing style and define content

Study the reference photograph (see Figure I.A.1) and decide how to organize the subject matter for your drawing. You can choose to draw a literal, realistic interpretation of the photograph, or use a loose, spontaneous style where the elements are abstracted and simplified.

Create a drawing surface and apply a grid

When you begin sketching, start with a grid to help organize the different elements in your composition within the picture's frame. Then add perspective lines to help you accurately sketch a template.

The following example is a realistic style drawing with proportions based on the original photo and uses a 4×6-inch drawing surface. By overlaying a simple grid on the reference photo and a corresponding one on your Photoshop file, it becomes easier to draw to scale and place elements accurately.

1. Open Photoshop and choose **File➡New**. Set file values to Width 6 inches, Height 4 inches, Resolution 300 dpi, Mode Grayscale, and Contents White.

2. Choose **File➡Preferences➡Guides & Grid**; set Gridline every 2 inches with 2 subdivisions (see Figure I.A.2). This preference setting displays your drawing surface in six square sections, each subdivided into four smaller squares. Choose **View➡Show Grid** if the grid is not visible.

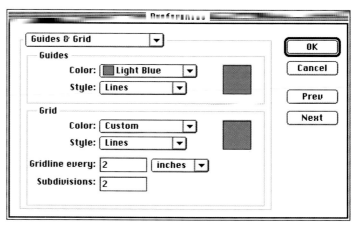

Figure I.A.2
The Guides & Grid dialog box

3. Turn off (remove the check mark) the Snap to Grid feature from the View menu.

If you were working with an original photo, you would draw corresponding gridlines on a tracing paper overlay taped to the back. Here you can simply refer to the grid drawn over the photo for this lesson (see Figure I.A.3).

Make a new layer

Create a special layer for the template that you can turn off and on as needed to view your work. To do this, choose **Layer➡New➡Layer**. Name this layer *Template*.

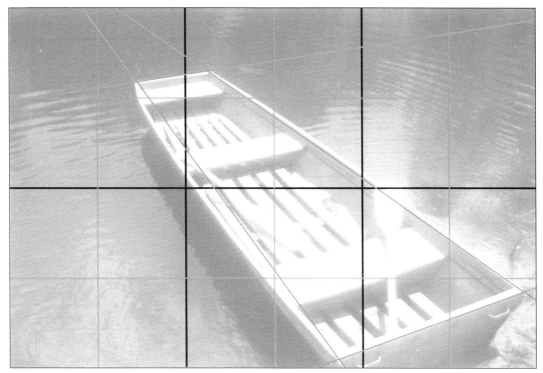

Figure I.A.3
A reference grid and perspective guides have been drawn over the photo for you.

Make perspective lines

Notice where the perspective lines drawn along the front, back, and sides of the boat in Figure I.A.3 fall within the grid squares. Draw corresponding lines for your template to assist in drawing the boat:

1. Choose a light gray (R175, G175, B175) as the default color. This is done by clicking the top-left color square at the bottom of the Photoshop toolbox. When the Color Picker dialog box opens, enter the values above for Red, Green, and Blue, and the color changes to the suggested light gray.

2. Press **N** to change to the Line tool. Double-click the Line tool and set Line Width to 2 pixels.

3. Click and drag lines to anchor the boat's corners at the same angles as those on the reference photo (see Figure I.A.4).

Figure I.A.4
Create a perspective grid.

Choose a pencil

Next, set the size and color of the pencil you want to use:

1. Switch to the Pencil tool by pressing **P**. Double-click the Pencil icon, or press **Return** (Macintosh) or **Enter** (Windows) to display the Pencil Options palette and choose Normal, 100% Opacity.

2. Choose **Window➡Show Brushes**. Choose the 2-pixel brush, which is the second from the left, top row.

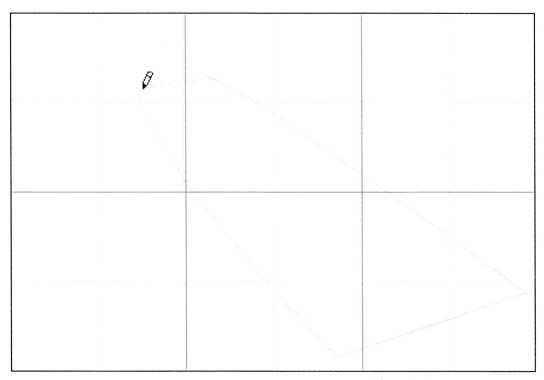

Rough in the basic shape of the boat

With the Pencil tool, loosely sketch the basic contour of the boat using a series of straight lines. To draw your lines, position the cursor, click to start your line, press the **Shift** key, move your mouse, and click again when you want the line to end. Release the mouse button to complete the line (see Figure I.A.5).

Always hold down **Shift** to keep the lines straight. Use short lines that begin and end where they intersect the gridlines. As you outline the boat, notice how its left side arches out beyond the perspective guide you drew earlier. Begin to get a feel for the boat's volume, the spacing of the seats, placement of the oars, and the angle from which the viewer is looking. Continue until you reach a level of detail similar to that shown in Figure I.A.6.

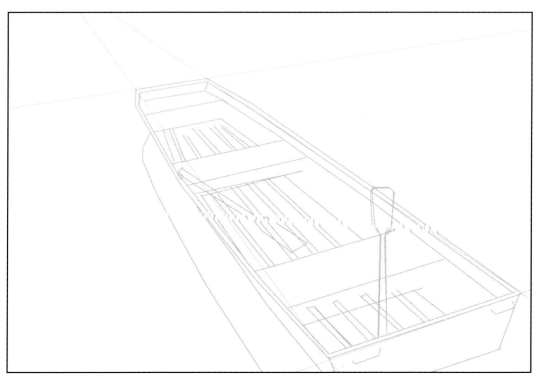

Figure I.A.6
Make straight lines by holding the Shift key while you rough in the boat's shape and major details.

Save your file

If you haven't done so already, save your drawing. You can call it *Boat 1*.

Now it's time to add more refined pencil and brush strokes, with different values and textures. Build up your drawing with curved, freehand, and crosshatch strokes. You work with the Paintbrush, following curved paths defined with the Pen tool.

Define curved lines

Use the Pen tool to define the curve for strokes that outline the shape of the boat more realistically than the straight lines you've worked with so far:

1. Make a new layer, named *Pencil strokes*, and zoom in to a magnified view of the boat's top-left corner.

2. Hide the grid. (Choose **View➥Hide Grid**.)

3. Select the Pen tool by pressing **P**.

4. Position the cursor where you want the curve to begin and hold down the mouse button. The first anchor point appears. Drag the mouse to reveal a direction line from the starting point. The length of the direction line determines the shape and direction of the curve. (see Figure I.A.7).

5. Click the mouse at the position where you want the line to end and drag out another handle before releasing the mouse button (see Figure I.A.8).

You can adjust the curve of the line by pressing the **Command** key (Macintosh) or the **Ctrl** key (Windows), which changes the cursor to the Direct Selection tool. Point to the handles on the direction lines or on the curved line and drag to adjust the curve until it's in the correct position.

Draw a stroke along the work path

After drawing a path, you can stroke it with the Pencil or Paintbrush tool, creating a line along the path using the tool's current size and color settings. The Paintbrush produces better results here because it has anti-aliasing, making its edges smoother than those made with the Pencil.

1. Change the foreground color to a darker gray (R121, G121, B121).

2. Double-click the Paintbrush tool and make sure that the palette shows Normal, 100% opacity, no fade, and no wet edges. Open the Brushes palette and choose the smallest brush shape in the second row. You are now ready to draw on the new layer.

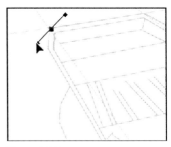

Figure I.A.7
Place a work path point by clicking once where you want the path to begin and then dragging out a direction handle.

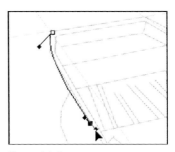

Figure I.A.8
Continue the work path to outline the boat's shape.

Figure I.A.9
The Paths palette.

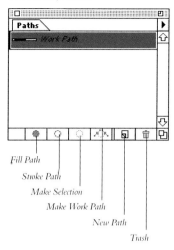

Fill Path
Stroke Path
Make Selection
Make Work Path
New Path
Trash

3. Choose **Window➡Show Paths** to open the Paths palette (see Figure I.A.9). Click the Stroke Path icon, which is second from the left on the bottom of the palette. The path becomes a stroked line in the color and brush thickness you have set.

4. Click the small trash can on the bottom right of the Paths palette to delete the path and its handles. A confirmation box appears, and when you choose **OK**, only the stroke is left behind.

5. Repeat the process until the outline of the boat, its seats, and the oars are redrawn with darker, thicker, curved lines. Turn the template layer off from time to time to check your progress. Build up the outline detail to a level similar to that shown in Figure I.A.10.

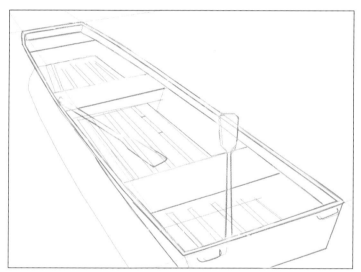

Figure I.A.10
Follow the template and outline the shape of the entire boat.

Next, using a crosshatching technique, begin to fill in the sides of the boat, shadows, and other details. Start by making some random pencil strokes; then clone them and lay them down over one another.

Make strokes for crosshatching

Laying down crosshatch strokes one at a time would be tedious in Photoshop, especially using a mouse. The method described in this section enables you to make a set of strokes that you can quickly apply to the drawing. To achieve more realistic looking pencil strokes, use the Paintbrush tool rather than the Pencil tool.

Figure I.A.11
Create a series of short pencil strokes that fade from darker to lighter.

1. Create a new layer and title it *Crosshatch*.

2. Choose a dark gray (R70, G70, B70) for the foreground color, and a lighter gray (R210, G210, B210) for the background color.

3. Double-click the Paintbrush tool or press **Return** (Macintosh) or **Enter** (Windows) to open the Paintbrush Options palette. Set Opacity at 70%, check the Fade box, enter **100** for the number of steps, and change Transparent to Background.

4. Open the Brushes palette. (Press palette shortcut key **F5**.) Choose the smallest (top-left) brush tip for your pencil.

5. Magnify your view to 100%, and just to the left of the boat make several short, overlapping strokes running in the same general direction, similar to those shown in Figure I.A.11. Use **Shift** to yield straight lines and vary the line angles slightly. Start half the strokes from left to right, and the other half from right to left to balance the fading effect.

Figure I.A.12
Create several sets of strokes at different angles for crosshatching.

Add strokes in other directions

Now make three or four more sets of strokes at different angles:

1. Select the first set of strokes with the Marquee tool. Copy the selection, paste it, and choose **Layer➥Transform➥Rotate**. Click a handle and drag to rotate the selection. Then click inside the selection and drag to move it next to the first set of strokes and press **Return** (Macintosh) or **Enter** (Windows).

2. Pasting an element adds a new layer to your file each time. Choose **Layer➥Merge Down** or press **Command-E** (Macintosh) or **Ctrl-E** (Windows) to combine the newly pasted strokes on the same layer with the original.

Continue to paste, rotate, and position strokes and merge layers until you have four or five sets of strokes at different angles in the layer called Crosshatch (see Figure I.A.12).

Fill areas with crosshatch strokes

Begin to fill in areas with crosshatching by using the Rubber Stamp tool to pick up a "brush" with crosshatch strokes and laying them down where you want them. You can fill areas darker or lighter by varying the opacity on the Rubber Stamp Options palette. Use 100% for dark areas such as shadows, and lesser percentages for lighter areas or highlights.

1. Open the Brushes palette and choose the 100-pixel diameter, soft-edged brush.

2. Press **S** to open the Rubber Stamp tool, and press **Return** (Macintosh) or **Enter** (Windows) to open the Rubber Stamp Options palette. Set the Opacity indicator to the percentage of darkness you want (a higher percentage yields a darker color), and choose the Clone (non-aligned) option.

3. Position the cursor over an area of the strokes you've drawn and holding down the **Option** key (Macintosh) or **Alt** key (Windows), click to pick up the strokes.

4. Use the Pen tool as you did earlier, but this time completely outline the area of the drawing you want to fill (such as the shadow under a seat). Click the **Make Selection** icon (third from the left) at the bottom of the Paths palette.

5. Press **S** for the Rubber Stamp tool again and click and drag inside the selected area to build up the crosshatch strokes (see Figure I.A.13).

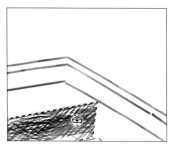

Figure I.A.13
Build up an area of crosshatch strokes with the Rubber Stamp tool.

Continue the process of holding down **Option** or **Alt** while picking up lines from different areas of the sample and then overlaying strokes in an area until you build up the detail you want. Use different Opacity settings for darker or lighter colors. For instance, you could use 35% for the boat's seats, 55% for the inside of the boat's side, and 100% for the shadows under the seats. In this way, you can gradually create different values for the boat's surfaces and shadows. Zoom in to closer levels of magnification, select smaller areas with the Pen tool, and finish filling in the drawing.

Lighten or darken areas in your drawing

You can use Photoshop's Dodge tool to lighten areas in your drawing that may have become too dark. Choose the tool by pressing **O**, and continue to press **O** if you first see the Sponge or Burn tool. (The Dodge tool looks like a lollipop.) Practice dragging the Dodge tool over the areas that you think are too dark. Use a large, soft-edged brush and a low Exposure setting of less than 20% to gradually apply the lightening effect. You may want to select part of your drawing to restrict the effects of the Dodge tool to a defined area.

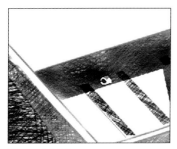

Figure I.A.14
Use the Toning tool, Burn, to
darken areas.

If you want to darken some areas, change the Dodge tool to the Burn tool by pressing **O** again or using the drop-down menu in the Toning Tools Options palette. The cursor changes to a hand, and as you pass the hand over an area, the area darkens (see Figure I.A.14). If you choose a low exposure setting, this effect is more gradual and easier to control.

Add final detail

Now add some final detail lines to polish your drawing. Create a new layer called *Fine lines*. Turn off the Template layer to view your drawing without the guidelines. Look over your drawing, find areas that need more detail, and use any of the methods you have learned in this lesson to add it. You can vary the size of the Paintbrush, as well as the color, ranging anywhere from black to white.

Adjust the opacity of layers

Turn off (but do not delete) the Template layer and adjust the opacity levels of the other layers to optimize the look of your drawing. For instance, you may want to lighten or even eliminate the Pencil strokes layer if your crosshatching has been careful and detailed. Try different settings and combinations until you are satisfied. To change the transparency of a layer, move the slider on the Layer Options palette.

Make a file for output

Save your file for later lessons in this book. Then choose **Save As**, and and give the file copy a different name. Delete the Template layer and merge the remaining layers by selecting **Layers➡Flatten Image**. Choose **Save As** again, and this time scroll down to select the TIFF format. This file is now ready to be printed or imported into a page layout program. Its level of detail is adequate for printing at up to 150% size on a 300 or 600 dpi laser printer or at 100% if you're using a higher resolution imagesetter.

Now you have created a drawing that looks like it was made with careful pencil strokes. As you gain more control of the Photoshop tools, you can apply this effect and many others in numerous different drawings. You can proceed to the next drawing lesson, which shows you how to draw a self portrait in charcoal, or move ahead to Part II, where you learn how to paint the drawing of the boat you just did in a water-color style.

Self-portrait by Barbara Kordesh

Part I: Lesson B   Drawing a face in "charcoal"

Finding a model to draw is as easy as looking in the mirror, and in this lesson you'll draw a self-portrait in "charcoal."

Why not simply apply the Charcoal artistic filter to a photograph? Filtering photographs can be a tantalizing way to make a drawing, but the real beauty of a charcoal drawing comes from the individuality that is expressed as each stroke is added to the image. Take a look at Georges Seurat's charcoal studies or the haunting self-portraits Käthe Kollwitz

Art concepts

The basic shape of the head

Proportioning the head

Positioning facial features

Point of view

Lighting

Expression

Compositional placement

Line and pattern

Surface texture

Photoshop tools and features

Paintbrush

Brush options

Eraser

Grid

Guidelines

Blur

did as a grieving mother, and you'll see the real power of a charcoal drawing to engage the viewer.

Photoshop's tools and features suggest such traditional drawing techniques as charcoal, carbon pencil, and graphite, but in reality the end result is not the same. Although for convenience's sake we use the term "charcoal," charcoal is, after all, a dusty medium that dates back to prehistoric cave drawings. For us, charcoal techniques serve rather as an inspiration to create a work that uses a variety of textures and tonal densities to achieve a certain expressive quality.

Creating a self-portrait is a personal means of artistic expression, and you can learn a lot about the face you present to the world—which you might not otherwise see. It's best not to work from a photograph because you can miss details and your work will reflect someone else's point of view. Instead, set up a mirror next to your computer and use it for reference to study your face.

Figure I.B.1
Finding a subject

Gather materials and set conditions

Gather these materials: a portable mirror large enough to reflect your head and shoulders, an eight- by ten-inch sheet of acetate (a transparent plastic film available at art supply stores), masking tape, a ruler, and a permanent fine-point marker.

Set up the mirror next to your computer in a position that enables you to work comfortably as you make a drawing of your face in Photoshop. Placing the mirror at arm's length from your face is a good distance.

If you don't have room for a mirror next to your computer, improvise. You can try taping the acetate on a remote mirror, tracing the outline of your head and facial features, removing the acetate from the mirror, and placing it next to your computer. This, however, isn't an ideal solution. You'll probably find it difficult to trace your reflection, and you'll need to return to the mirror often to check shading and other details.

Draw a grid on the acetate

Use the ruler and fine-point marker to divide the surface of the acetate into a grid as shown in Figure I.B.2. Make three vertical and four horizontal solid rules spaced two inches apart. Then add dotted lines halfway between each solid rule. Now, tape the acetate to the mirror, which should frame your face when you're sitting comfortably to observe and work.

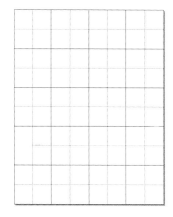

Figure I.B.2
Draw a grid on the acetate using solid and dotted lines.

Set lighting conditions

Decide whether you want to work in natural or artificial light. If you're using artificial light, find a lamp that can cast interesting shadows on your face without creating unduly harsh highlights or excessively dark areas. Ideal lighting would be from one side, just above and to the front of your head. A small clip-on lamp, attached to the top of the mirror, might work well.

If you decide to use natural light, select a time of day that will be available to you for several work sessions. Your self-portrait will probably take more than one sitting, and it can be difficult to match the same tonal and shadow patterns of your first work session if you have to work at a different time of day.

Choose a view and facial expression

Decide between a frontal or side view (profile) for your portrait. Will you tilt your head or keep it straight? What about wearing a hat, eyeglasses, jewelry, or other accessories?

Try a variety of poses and facial expressions until you discover one you want to illustrate. Try on looks reflecting different emotions: joy, sadness, thoughtfulness, bemusement, and anger. Make your expression as comfortable and natural as possible.

Because you'll be referring to the position of your features in relation to the grid as you draw, choose an intersection of the grid lines where you can always align a portion of your face. Place the tip of your nose, for example, at the point where two lines intersect, or make sure your ears are completely contained by particular grid squares. That way, if your work is interrupted, you can come back to the mirror and quickly reposition your image in the same place.

Figure I.B.3
Study the skeleton before drawing the head.
(Photo courtesy of Digital Stock, *www.digitalstock.com*.)

Prepare a drawing surface

To create a drawing surface, open Photoshop and, in Grayscale mode, create a new file at 300 dpi that measures five inches tall and four inches wide. Then apply a grid, add a new layer to begin drawing, and follow the next steps.

1. Choose **File➡Preferences➡Guides & Grid**. Set the Gridline at every inch with 2 subdivisions. This grid is exactly half as large as the one on your acetate.

2. Select **View➡Show Grid**, and make sure the Snap to Grid feature is turned off.

3. Create a new layer and name it *Template*.

Sketch in the head, neck, and shoulders

As you draw your self portrait, refer to Figures I.B.3, I.B.4, and I.B.5. They show the skeletal and muscle structure of the head, and a linear 3D model of the head.

Use the default foreground and background colors of black and white to create the initial shape of your head and shoulders. Then make black the foreground color in the Photoshop toolbox. Press **P** to open the Paintbrush tool and press **Return** (Macintosh) or **Enter** (Windows) to open the Paintbrush Options palette. Set Mode as Normal and Opacity at 100%. Open the Brushes palette (**Window➡Show Brushes**) and choose the smallest (1-pixel) brush.

Magnify the view of your file to the largest size that fits your screen, still showing the entire canvas. Press **Tab** to hide the toolbar and other dialog boxes.

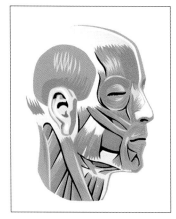

Figure I.B.4
Understanding facial musculature helps when drawing portraits. (Photo courtesy of Corel Corporation, *www.corel.com*.)

Figure I.B.5
A 3D model of the head. (Model courtesy of Viewpoint Data Labs, Inc., *www.viewpoint.com*.)

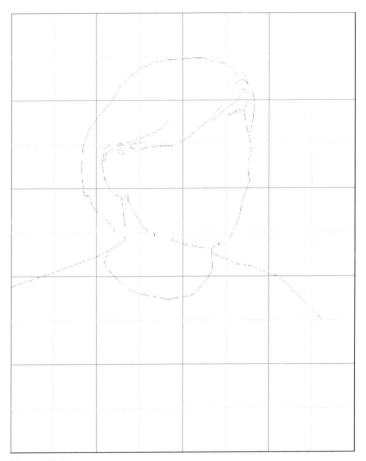

Figure I.B.6
Block in the outline of your head, neck, and shoulders using the grid
for reference.

Now, begin with the basic shape of your head, jawbone, neck, and shoulders by making short straight lines with the Paintbrush Click where you want the line to begin and, holding the **Shift** key to constrain the strokes to a straight line, click again where the line is to end. If you make a mistake and want to erase a portion of the lines you've drawn, press **E** to change to the Eraser tool, erase as needed, and press **B** again to switch back to the Paintbrush. Using the grid as a reference, outline your complete head and shoulders similar to Figure I.B.6.

Block in your facial features

Switch to the Pen tool by pressing **P**. First, make a curved line from the eyebrow to the top of the ear, as shown in Figure I.B.7. Make sure you have the 1-pixel brush tip selected, and, at the bottom of the Paths palette, click the second circle from the left to stroke the curved line. Next, click the palette's small trashcan to delete the path and click **OK**. Then draw another curve from the tip of the nose to the lobe of the ear, stroke, and delete the path. You'll notice that the nose and ear are about the same length. Make a third curved line from the top of the head to the chin to indicate the position of the nose.

Now switch back to the Paintbrush by pressing **B,** and block in your eyebrows, nose, eyes, ears, mouth, and other facial features. Work without holding the **Shift** key so that you can achieve Paintbrush strokes with subtle curves. You'll probably want to erase some of the straight lines from your initial blocking in and replace them with more accurate curved lines. In addition to using the Eraser tool, you can press **X** to switch the Paintbrush color to white (if that's your background color) to paint over some of the previous strokes, and then press **X** again to return the Paintbrush to black.

Lighten the template

Because you will use the drawing you just made as a template for placing more refined charcoal strokes, it must be lightened so that the effects of your shading and charcoal strokes can be seen more easily. Select **Image➡Adjust➡Brightness/Contrast** and increase Brightness by 100% and Contrast by 50% in the dialog box. This changes your template drawing from black on white to a lighter gray on white.

Make a new layer for shading

Create another new layer and name it *Shading*. You can use this layer to create areas of shadow and highlight, which will begin to give your portrait a more realistic, dimensional appearance.

Figure I.B.7
Block in three curved lines to guide the placement of facial features, and then use the Paintbrush to add the features.

Use large brushes to create shading

Open the Brushes palette and choose a 35-pixel brush. Click the black square representing the foreground color, and when the color picker appears, make the foreground color a light gray (R180, G180, B180). Click **OK**.

Now change the Opacity of your Paintbrush to 20%, and begin painting in the shadowed areas of your face. The emphasis here is on defining the planes of the face with the shadows you see in the mirror's reference image.

If you build up an area with too many strokes and it becomes too dark, switch to the Eraser tool by pressing **E**. Using the Eraser Options palette, set the Opacity to 50% and Mode to Paintbrush. Choose a 35-pixel brush tip on the Brushes palette, and lighten the dark areas. Continue to define shadows until your drawing looks similar to Figure I.B.8.

Figure I.B.8
Use a large paintbrush with 20% Opacity and a light gray color to suggest shadows on different planes of your face.

Make charcoal strokes

Now add detail to your drawing. First make another new layer and name it *Charcoal*. Change your brush tip to the 1-pixel brush, and on the Brush Options palette set Opacity at 50%. Click the Foreground Color box and when the Color Picker appears, enter a value of 80 for each of R, G, and B, and click OK. This makes the foreground color a dark gray.

Use short strokes, following the template you drew earlier. Outline your head and shoulders, and add your facial features. Make strokes close to one another to suggest shadowed areas.

Switch to the Smudge tool by pressing **U**, set Pressure at 30%, and choose a brush tip from 1 to 5 pixels. Drag the Smudge tool randomly over the strokes to smear them and make them look more like real charcoal. Continue to add and smudge strokes until you have reached a level of detail similar to Figure I.B.9.

Figure I.B.9
Make 1-pixel, dark-gray strokes with the Paintbrush, and use the Smudge tool to blend them.

Figure I.B.10
Combine layers and use the Toning tools to even out strokes and shadows.

Add final touch-up

Now that you've reached the final stage, you can turn off the Grid and hide the *Template* layer by clicking its eye icon on the Layers palette. Add any final charcoal strokes, paying close attention to your eyes, ears, nose, and mouth. When you're satisfied with the appearance of the charcoal strokes, press **Command-E** (Macintosh) or **Ctrl-E** (Windows) to combine the *Charcoal* layer with the *Shading* layer below it.

Next, lighten or darken areas of strokes and shadows. Select the Toning tools by pressing **O**. Switch between the Dodge tool (to lighten) and the Burn tool (to darken) by pressing **O** again. Choose a brush tip of 1 to 5 pixels for tight areas and larger brushes for large areas. Set Exposure at 30% on the Toning Tools Options palette. Drag the Dodge or Burn tools over areas to lighten or darken them as needed. The finished drawing shown in Figure I.B.10 is smoothed out this way; the eyes are made more dominant with the Burn tool, and the shadows are lightened with the Dodge tool.

Create a sandstone texture

Next, add a sandstone texture to simulate the dusty, broken character of real charcoal strokes. Select **Filter➡Texture➡Texturizer**. When the Texturizer palette opens, change the mode to Sandstone on the pull-down menu. Set Scaling at 60%, Relief at 6, and Top for light direction. Click **OK** to apply the filter. Your drawing will look something like Figure I.B.11.

Figure I.B.11
Add a sandstone texture to the drawing.

Figure I.B.12
Eraser strokes begin to reveal the drawing below the white layer.

Add a layer of white and erase strokes

The Texturizer filter created a uniform sandstone texture on the entire drawing. By adding a layer of white and carefully erasing it in certain areas, you can make the texture appear more realistic and varied.

Add a new layer, and fill it with white. Lower the layer's opacity to 90% on the Layers palette, so you can just see the outline of your portrait. Press **E** to switch to the Eraser tool. On the Eraser Options palette, lower Opacity to 60%, and choose Paintbrush mode. Select the 5-pixel diameter, soft-edged brush tip, and begin to erase away the layer of white, as shown in Figure I.B.12.

Continue to erase the white until you have revealed as much of the underlying layer as you like.

Now that you've seen how easy it is to draw a self-portrait, you might want to persuade someone else to model for you. Apply the same principles you've learned about shape of the head, proportion, facial expressions, shading, and highlighting.

When you finish this lesson, save two copies: a final black-and-white sketch and a work copy. You can proceed to the next drawing lesson where you'll draw a still life of lemons, or to Part II to learn how to create a palette and colorize your portrait in a pastel fashion. In later lessons, you'll make oil painting and scratchboard versions of your portrait.

Part I: Lesson C **Airbrushing three lemons**

In the first two lessons, you learned how to draw with pencil and charcoal effects. In this lesson, you use the Airbrush tool to paint a still life.

Part of the look of airbrush illustration is the absence of hard lines around shapes. Instead, silhouettes are defined by blending and contrast, in graduated tones ranging from very dark to very light.

You can emulate the effects of a real airbrush when using Photoshop by making selections and masks to create the electronic equivalent

Art concepts

Figure–ground relationship

Additive process

Receding space

Silhouette

Grouping

Volume

Shape

Value

Texture

Photoshop tools and features

Airbrush

Marquee tools

Layers

Masks

Custom brushes

Toning tools

of "friskets," which block out specific areas in the traditional airbrush illustration process.

When using the airbrush, artists usually work from dark to light. This means that the areas that will be the darkest are painted first, with successive coats adding to the previously applied ones. As you paint, a pressure setting of 10% or less gives you more precise control to balance "paint" and "air,"

In later lessons, you colorize your drawing and expand its canvas so that you can add elements. Finally, you render your painting in an impressionist style.

Build a still life composition

Position three lemons on a large sheet of white paper with two in the foreground and the third behind them. Set up a desk lamp so that it illuminates the composition and creates clearly defined light and dark areas. Adjust the light's angle so that it emphasizes the texture on the skin of the lemons and casts shadows from the first two lemons onto the third one.

You may want to set up your still life in the morning and observe it under different lighting conditions during the day. Choose a time to do your drawing when the shadows and reflections are most dramatic.

Create a drawing surface

Open a new file 6 inches wide and 4 inches high, with 300dpi resolution, Grayscale mode, and white contents. Apply a grid as you did in Part I, Lesson A. Select **File➥Preferences➥Guides & Grid** with a gridline set every 2 inches with 2 subdivisions.

It's more difficult to visualize a grid placed over the subject matter when you're drawing from real life. Make sure that you always use the same point of view whenever looking at the subject matter: look at it from the same distance and perspective each time you refer to it for drawing the individual elements.

Create an outline for the first lemon

Although a lemon is roughly oval in shape, it needs to be drawn with an irregular outline. The easiest approach is to start with a perfectly defined oval and add or subtract from the oval to create an irregular shape. To prepare the file, choose **Layer➥New➥ Layer** and name the new layer *Lemon 1*.

1. Activate the Marquee tool by pressing **M**. Press the **Return** key (Macintosh) or **Enter** key (Windows) to open the Marquee Options palette. Choose Elliptical for Shape and select Constrained Aspect Ratio for Style. A good ratio for the average lemon's proportions is 1.25 wide, 1 high. Make sure that Feather is 0 pixels and Anti-aliased is unchecked.

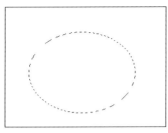

Figure I.C.1
Define the lemon's basic shape by drawing an oval with the elliptical Marquee tool.

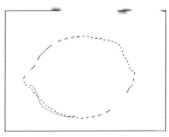

Figure I.C.2
Add irregularity to the outline with the Lasso tool, adding and subtracting from the oval to refine the lemon's outline.

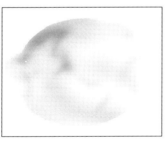

Figure I.C.3
Build up contrasting areas of dark and light with the Airbrush.

2. Draw an oval to describe the basic shape of the first lemon. Don't worry if the oval is not at the right angle; you can adjust it later. Pay attention to the grid to determine the correct size for the lemon.

3. Switch to the Lasso tool by pressing **L**, with Feather at 0 pixels and Anti-aliased unchecked.

4. Click inside the oval, hold down the **Shift** key and drag outside the oval to add irregularity to its outline. Subtract areas from the previously drawn oval by holding the **Option** key (Macintosh) or the **Alt** key (Windows) as you drag from outside the oval to the inside to delete portions. (see Figure I.C.1 and Figure I.C.2).

When you are satisfied with the lemon's shape, choose **Selection➥Save Selection** so that you can select the outline of this lemon later when necessary.

Choose your Airbrush settings

Switch to the Airbrush tool by pressing **A**. Use a brush with Mode set to Normal on the Airbrush Options palette and the Pressure at 10%. Choose **Window➥Show Brushes** to open the Brushes palette and select a brush tip with a 200-pixel diameter, 0% Hardness, and 25% Spacing. (If you didn't create this brush in a previous lesson, make a new brush with these specifications.)

Change the foreground color to a light gray (R140, G140, B140).

Fill the selected area with Airbrush strokes

Begin to build up the shadowed areas by spraying the brush inside the selected area defining the lemon. Using such a light gray and a low pressure setting, it takes several strokes to build up the right values. Don't worry if you paint gray into areas that should be lighter; you can spray white later to lighten those portions (see Figure I.C.3).

To get the darkest value from the stroke along the edge of the lemon, click and drag the Airbrush just outside the selected lemon. This way, the part of the stroke that would fade to a lighter value does not show on the lemon. Switch to smaller brushes of 100- or 65-pixel diameters to add smaller shadows.

Define a new brush tip for the lemon's texture

Follow these steps to define a new brush tip that you can use to add texture to the lemon's skin:

1. Select the soft-edged, 5-pixel diameter brush tip (first on the second row), set Pressure at 60% on the Airbrush Options palette, and change the foreground color to black.

2. Deselect the lemon shape and spray a number of small dots like those shown here outside the lemon, to fill about a 1-inch square (see Figure I.C.4).

3. Switch back to the Marquee tool by pressing **M**, hold down **Shift**, and draw a circle around a group of the dots to select them.

4. Choose **Define Brush** from the Brushes palette menu. This adds a new brush with the dot pattern you just created.

5. Delete the dots from which the brush was made so that the only remaining paint on the layer is that of the lemon.

Figure I.C.4
Fill a 1-inch square with 5-pixel black Airbrush sprays and use them to define a new brush tip.

Paint texture on the lemon's skin

Reload the lemon's channel to make it an active selection. Change back to a gray color (R100, G100, B100), press **A** to switch to the Airbrush tool, and choose the new dot pattern brush tip. Set Pressure at 30% and use this brush to apply texture to the lemon's skin by clicking (but not dragging) in places where you want the texture to appear.

Set the background color to white (R255, G255, B255) and press **X** to switch the foreground and background colors. Add white texture in the areas where the light reflects, using the new dot pattern brush. When painting with white, increase the Pressure setting on the Airbrush Options palette to 60%. If you paint too much white in an area, switch back to gray by pressing **X**, lowering Pressure to 30% and adding texture back in (see Figure I.C.5).

Figure I.C.5
Use a custom brush tip to paint texture on the lemon's skin.

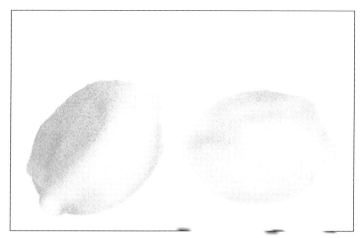

Figure I.C.6
After you paint the second lemon, rotate it into position and save
the selection.

Paint and position the second lemon

Select **Layer➡New➡Layer** and name the new layer *Lemon 2*.
Follow the same procedure you used to create the first lemon,
using the elliptical Marquee and Lasso tools to define an irregular
oval shape. If your second lemon is longer or shorter than the
first, change the Constrained Aspect Ratio accordingly.
In the preceding example, the second lemon is slightly longer
and has a ratio of Width: 1.3, Height: 1. Be sure to save the outline of the second lemon by choosing **Selection➡Save Selection**. Next, use the Airbrush as before to paint the shadows and
later the textures.

When you are satisfied with the appearance of the second lemon,
choose **Layer➡Transform➡Rotate**. A box with handles sur-
rounds the lemon. Click one of the handles and drag the lemon
to set it at the proper angle (see Figure I.C.6). Note that after you
have rotated the lemon, when you choose Load Selection to make
it active, its former position is selected. You can correct this by
pressing W and clicking the Magic Wand tool in the white area
surrounding the lemon to select the layer's background. Then
choose **Select➡Inverse** followed by **Select➡Save Selection**
to create yet another channel.

Paint and position the third lemon

Make a third layer named *Lemon 3*. Because this third lemon is behind the other two, create a mask so that the parts that should be hidden by the other lemons do not show through.

1. Choose **Select➡Load Selection** once for the first lemon and again for the second. When loading the second selection, choose **Add to Selection** in the Load Selection dialog box.

2. With both the lemons selected, choose **Layer➡Add Layer Mask➡Hide Selection**. This means that the selected areas (the first and second lemons) will be masked out when you paint the third lemon.

3. On the Layer palette, haick the Layer thumbnail, which is directly to the left of the Layer mask thumbnail. The Lemon 3 layer is now active for painting.

Follow the procedure used for the previous two lemons to outline and paint the third one. Be sure to save its selection because it will be needed later.

This lemon should be painted darker than the other lemons because the lemons in the front are casting shadows onto the one in the back. You get a good sense of how dark the third lemon should be when the two lemons in front begin to stand out against the lemon in the back (see Figure I.C.7).

Figure I.C.7
The third lemon should be darker than the two in front of it because of the shadows they cast on it.

Add a layer for the paper and paint shadows

Choose **Layer➡New➡Layer** and name the result *Paper*. Load the selections for all three lemons by checking **Add to Selection** in the Load Selection dialog box each time you add a lemon. Choose **Layer➡Add Layer Mask➡Hide Selection** to block out the lemons from the painting you will do now, and click the Layer thumbnail directly to the left of the Layer mask thumbnail.

Create a 400-pixel brush with 0% Hardness and 25% Spacing. Change your foreground color to another level of gray (R140, G140, B140). On the Airbrush Options palette, set Mode to Normal and Pressure to 10%. In the background, begin making broad strokes that correspond to the shadows cast by the lamp on your subject. Notice how the shadows are darker near the bottom of the lemons; switch to the 200-pixel brush and build up these shadows, as shown in Figure I.C.8.

Figure I.C.8
Use a large brush, from 200 to 400 pixels and airbrush in background shadows.

Increase contrast by using the Toning tools

After you've painted the shadows in the background, you can use the Dodge tool to lighten areas that are too dark or the Burn tool to darken light parts. These tools are particularly useful to darken shadows near the borders of the lemons (see Figure I.C.9) and to brighten areas to suggest reflected light. Press **O** to select these tools and to switch between them.

Figure I.C.9
The Dodge and Burn tools can be used to heighten contrast in your painting.

When using the Toning tools, choose a large, soft-edged brush and set Opacity at 30% or less to achieve subtle darkening or lightening effects. Switch to the different layers and load selections where appropriate to confine the toning to specific areas.

Add final detail

Now add final details, such as the stems or some blemishes, to finish your painting. Choose small brush tips, from 2 to 5 pixels in diameter, and a dark gray with Pressure set to 50% (see Figure I.C.10). Apply these details on the appropriate layers for each lemon.

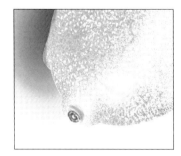

Figure I.C.10
Use a small brush tip, a dark gray color, and higher pressure setting to paint detail on the lemons.

Make a file for output

Save your file for later lessons. If you want to output the painting in grayscale, choose **Save As**, and give the file a new name. Merge the layers by selecting **Layers➡Flatten Image** and choose **Mode➡CMYK**. Choose **Save As** again, and this time scroll down to select the TIFF format. The file is now ready to be printed, or imported into a page layout program. Its level of detail is adequate for printing at up to 150% size on a 300 or 600dpi laser printer or at 100% if you're using a higher resolution imagesetter.

Illustrating with the Airbrush tool can add delicate shades of meaning to your imagery with its soft, blended look. The absence of hard edges on airbrushed objects makes them look more like they do in real life, and the shadows and reflections also add realism.

You can now proceed to the last lesson in Part I, where you learn to create an architectural illustration, or go to Part II, Lesson D where you'll bring to life the lemons you've just illustrated in black and white by adding color.

Part I: Lesson D   **Illustrating a door**

Artists have always been drawn to architecture as a subject for their paintings. The clean lines and well-defined planes of walls, roofs, windows, and doors make wonderful studies of light and shadow, color and form. The way the built environment interacts with nature adds further appeal.

Art concepts

Orthographic drawing

Measurement

Proportion

Point of view

Lighting

Surface texture

**Photoshop tools
and features**

Marquee

Paintbrush

Brush options

Eraser

Rulers

Gradients

Grid

Guidelines

This lesson uses one of architecture's most commonplace features: the door. Its simple form is easy to illustrate, and a picture of a door can carry a lot of emotional content. You can draw one of the doors shown here or find a real door and sketch or photograph it for reference. Of course, you can always draw a door from your imagination.

Photoshop's tools and features lend themselves well to architectural illustration because you can measure and draw perfectly straight horizontal, vertical, and angled lines. You can apply perspective, change lighting conditions, and repeat such details as bricks or window panes. The challenge for the fine artist is to strike a balance between precision and originality.

Start with a straight-on point of view to make drawing the door simpler. When you finish this lesson, save two copies: a final black-and-white sketch and a work copy.

Make photos or sketches for subject material

When you make your initial sketch or photograph of a door, be sure to do so with lighting conditions that will show as many of the door's features as possible. Study the door up close for details, such as handles or trim, and from a distance to make note of its surroundings.

Use the photo or sketch as a visual reference for this exercise. If you want to be precise, use a ruler to measure and work with a grid, but avoid scanning and tracing over the photo or sketch.

Open a new file

Open Photoshop and create a new file in Grayscale mode at 300 dpi. The example shown here uses a file that measures six inches tall and four inches wide. Adjust your file's measurements according to the size of the door you're drawing. Name the file *Door1*.

Apply a grid and add a new layer

It's advantageous to work with a file that measures in one-inch increments, such as four by six inches, because it's easier to apply a grid that will evenly divide the image into one-inch squares.

1. Choose **File➧Preferences➧Guides & Grid**, and choose measurements for your grid that correspond to those you made on your reference photo or sketch.

2. Select **View➧Show Grid**, and make sure the Snap to Grid feature is turned off.

3. Create a new layer and name it *Template*.

Figure I.D.1
Make guidelines for the outline of the door, using the grid for reference.

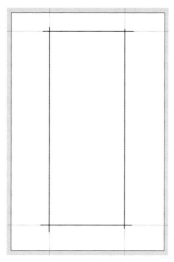

Figure I.D.2
Block in the door's outline with the Line tool, using the guidelines for reference.

Create guidelines and draw the door's outline

If guidelines are not visible, choose **View➡Show Guides**, and if rulers are hidden, choose **View➡Show Rulers**. Click in the top ruler and drag down to make a guideline for the bottom of the door, referring to the gridlines for correct placement. Drag another horizontal guideline from the top ruler to serve as a guideline for the top of the door. Then, from the ruler on the left, drag out two guidelines for the sides of the door (see Figure I.D.1).

Use the default foreground/background colors of black and white. Press **N** to choose the Line tool, and press **Return** (Macintosh) or **Enter** (Windows) to open the Line Tool Options palette. Use Normal mode, 100% Opacity, a 2-pixel Line Width, and turn off the Anti-aliased option.

Block in the outline of the door with the Line tool. Be sure to hold the **Shift** key so your lines will be perfectly horizontal or vertical. Don't worry about the lines going beyond the corners, because at this point you are only creating a template to trace over later (see Figure I.D.2).

Make more guidelines and add details

Continue to drag out guidelines to help in the placement of other features on the door, such as window panes, door handles, and decorative trim. As before, use the Line tool to sketch in the location of the door's other features. If there are curved features in your door, switch to the Pencil tool by pressing **Y**, and use a 1- or 2-pixel brush tip to sketch the curves (see Figure I.D.3).

If your door has repeating elements (such as the filigree in the bottom panels of the example drawing), you can draw the element once, select it with the Marquee tool, and then copy and paste it. The copy will appear in a new layer. Switch to the Move tool by pressing **V**, and hold the **Shift** key if you want to keep the element aligned, while you click the copy of the element and move it into place.

Note that the design on the right bottom panel of the example door is a mirror reflection of the one on the left. This was done by selecting the copy of the design on the right side, and choosing **Layer➡Transform➡Flip Horizontal**.

Create and fill a path for the door

Making and saving paths is an efficient way to define elements so you can isolate them later to add fills, shading, or other effects.

Hide both the Guidelines and the Gridlines by using the View pull-down menu. If your door's basic shape is rectangular, you can use the Marquee tool to make a path that defines its outline. Press **M** to change to the Marquee tool, and if the rectangular marquee isn't showing, continue pressing **M** until it is.

Using the template for reference, click down on the top-left corner of the door and drag a marquee to the bottom-right corner. Make this marquee into a path by clicking the fourth circle from the left (Make Work Path) on the bottom of the Paths palette (see Part I, Lesson A, Figure I.A.9).

After you make the selection into a path, choose **Save Path** from the Paths palette menu (click the arrow on the top right of the Paths palette to summon the menu).

Now make a new layer, call it *Base*, and move it below the *Template* layer by clicking and dragging its thumbnail onto the Layers palette. Then change to the Paths palette, and select the path for the outline of the door by clicking its thumbnail. Make it an active selection by clicking the Make Selection circle (third from the left on the bottom) of the palette.

Change the foreground color to a light gray by entering values of 200 for each of R, G, and B when the Color Picker opens. Click the first circle on the bottom of the Paths palette to fill the selection with gray.

Now change the foreground color back to black, and switch to the Pencil tool by pressing **Y**. Choose the second brush from the left in the top row of the Brushes palette, the 3-pixel brush tip. Click the Stroke Path circle (second from the left) on the bottom of the Paths palette to stroke the outside of the door with a 3-pixel pencil line (see Figure I.D.4).

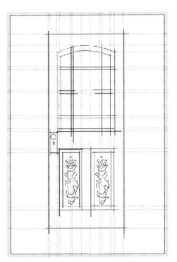

Figure I.D.3
Add the rest of the door's basic features to the template.

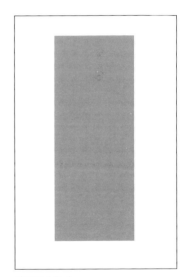

Figure I.D.4
Select the door's path, make it an active selection, fill with gray and stroke with a 3-pixel black line.

Figure I.D.5
Make paths for more complex features in the door.

Figure I.D.6
Use gradient fills to suggest light and shadows on the door's surface.

Make paths for other features of the door

Now you can begin to make and save paths for the various details in the door. If you're describing perfectly rectangular areas, you can use the Marquee tool. When you're describing curves or irregular shapes, you'll need to use the Pen tool.

You can change to the Pen tool by pressing **P**. For more instructions on using paths, see Part I, Lesson A. Outline the door's details, then make and save paths.

When you're creating paths for small details (such as the thin mullions between the panes of glass in this door), you may find it helpful to zoom in to a high level of magnification so that you have more control over the placement of the elements.

Paths for elements such as the scrollwork shown on the bottom of the door in Figure I.D.5 are more complicated to draw. If an element such as this repeats, you can draw the first one, then duplicate it. If you wish to create a mirror image, position the copy and flip it horizontally or vertically by choosing **Layer➡Free Transform**.

Create light and shadows with gradient fills

Gradients are found throughout nature, and their effects are also seen on architectural surfaces. Consider the smooth blends of colors in a sunset sky. The light from that sunset can be seen reflected in windowpanes or on the surfaces of walls and roofs.

Adding gradients to architectural illustrations makes them appear more realistic by creating the illusion of light. Load paths for your door and its features one at a time, and choose contrasting (dark/light) grays for foreground and background colors. Press **G** to switch to the Gradient tool. On the Gradient Options palette, set 50% or lower Opacity, and a Linear fill. Drag the cursor across the surface you want to fill, and it will become shaded from dark to light—or light to dark.

Use gradients in the same direction to suggest light falling on certain portions of the door. Use a gradient in the opposite direction to suggest shadows (see Figure I.D.6).

Fill the door's handle with gradients

Now load the path for the doorknob and make it an active selection. Begin by choosing the Gradient tool, and in the Gradient Tool Options palette, set the Type to Radial and Opacity at 50% or more. Use white for the foreground color and medium gray for the background. When you click in the circle that outlines the doorknob, the brightest part of the radial fill will start where you click and darken in the direction you drag.

In the example in Figure I.D.7, a soft, dark outline is in the center of the doorknob. You can create a similar effect by following these steps:

1. Load the path for the outline of the knob and make a new layer.

2. Choose **Select➥Modify➥Contract** to make the selection smaller. Enter a number of pixels for the contraction. You may need do this more than once because 16 pixels is the highest number you can enter, and that may not be enough to reduce the selection to the size you want.

3. Choose **Select➥Modify➥Border** to select the border of the circle. Enter a value of eight to 12 pixels for the border.

4. Choose **Feather** and enter a pixel value that is less than half your border size (otherwise, no selection can be made).

5. Change the foreground color to a dark gray and fill the selection. Then adjust layer Opacity to lighten the effect as desired.

The same effect used on the doorknob was also used on the doorplate behind it.

Finally, with selections for the knob and plate both active, add some texture with the Noise filter. Choose **Filter➥Noise➥Add Noise** and when the dialog box opens, enter a value of 12 or below, select Uniform distribution and click **OK**.

Figure I.D.7
Pay special attention to the door's handle because it is a focal point of the drawing.

Figure I.D.8
Use Layers and Masks to fill border areas with shadows and highlights.

Create the appearance of raised areas

You can create a sense of dimension to accentuate raised and recessed areas of the door. Here is how the window frame in this example was made to appear raised:

1. Create a new layer and name it *Shadows*. Load the path for the outside edge of the window frame and make it an active selection.

2. Choose **Select→Modify→Border**. Enter a value of 24. Choose **Select→Feather** and enter a value of 8. Fill the selection with dark gray.

3. Make a layer mask by selecting **Layer→Add Layer Mask→Reveal Selection**.

4. Duplicate the layer and name it *Highlights*. Then select the window frame again. Select the border and feather the edge with the same values as in Step 2. This time, fill with white, and again make a layer mask to reveal the selection.

5. Use the Eraser tool in Airbrush mode at 50% Opacity and carefully erase the dark areas on the top and left of the window frame in the Shadows layer. Erase the light areas on the bottom and right of the window frame on the Highlights area (see Figure I.D.8).

Create the appearance of recessed areas

The panels at the bottom of the door appear recessed by following the same steps as previously listed, with shadows and highlights applied in the opposite direction. That is, dark areas appear to the top and left, and light areas on the right and bottom (see Figure I.D.9).

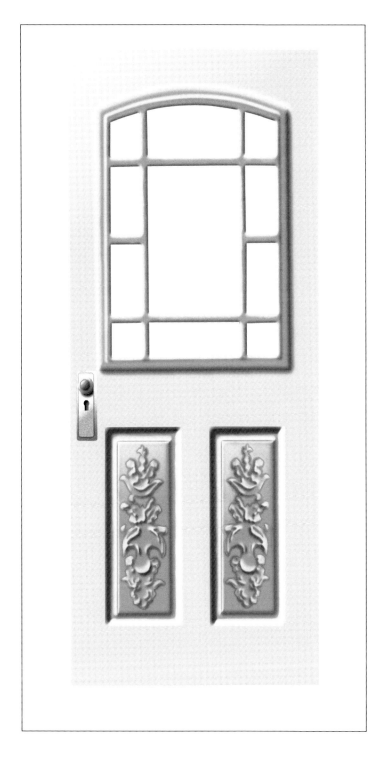

Figure I.D.9
Create recessed areas by switching
the positions of shadows and
highlights.

You've seen how easy it is to create architectural drawings using Photoshop's powerful tools for measurement, alignment, and selection. Gradients, layers, and masks help by facilitating shadows and highlights.

In later lessons, you'll add texture and color to your door to achieve even more realism, and then surround the door with more context so it can tell a story.

Part II: Lesson A Creating custom palettes

Color is the soul of a painting. When you're painting, you make conscious or unconscious color decisions based on many things. How many tubes of paint do you have, and what colors are they? What kind of atmosphere and mood do you want to create in your painting?

When you paint with Photoshop, your paint supply never runs out, and color choices are virtually unlimited. And you never have to clean your brushes! But such a blessing can also be a curse, leaving you overwhelmed and at a loss where to begin. How do you select just the right blue from a hundred thousand possibilities? As you learn in this lesson, the solution is to build a custom palette.

A custom palette narrows down the bewildering array of choices and can ensure that the colors you use are printable. You can keep a custom palette open next to your painting and easily switch colors with the click of a mouse.

You can build a custom palette by observing subjects in real life and adding the colors you see one by one, or you can load the color table of any Photoshop image and make a palette from the 256 swatches it displays.

Art concepts:

Atmosphere

Light

Emotion

Color combinations

Complementary colors

Adjacent colors

Expression

Hue

Value

**Photoshop tools
and features :**

Swatches

Color Picker

For example, you may want to paint a portrait using a color photograph of your subject for reference. You can scan the photo, open the scan in Photoshop, and use the file's color table as a palette that has the correct skin tones for your subject. Or, if you're painting a landscape scene of a fall day, you can start with a blank palette and individually select just the right range of oranges, reds, browns, and yellows — or whatever colors you want to use.

If you create a palette based on one of Photoshop's custom color systems, such as Trumatch, you ensure that your artwork can be accurately printed using the four-color process.

After you load or create a custom palette, save it for future use by placing it in the folder along with the palettes that come with Photoshop.

Building the color atmosphere

When you build a palette for any composition, you want to create the right color atmosphere. If you're painting an outdoor scene, consider the geographical location of your scene. Is it in a temperate or tropical climate? What is the season, the weather conditions, and time of day? Is the sun rising or setting, or is the scene bathed in moonlight?

If you're painting a subject that's indoors, what kind of light is in the room? It could range from candlelight (with warm yellow and orange glows) to fluorescent (a harsh, blue-green cast) or incandescent (yellow-orange). Or the light could be the sun filtering through a window (blue from the ultraviolet rays). It could be harsh and direct (casting deep shadows), or soft and muted (yielding a smoother range of tones).

It's completely up to you, the artist, to create the right atmosphere for your painting. Paint exactly what you see, or use your imagination and play with the effects of color and atmosphere.

Adding emotional colors

Color can also evoke a mood by expressing your personal emotions. To portray a feeling of serenity, you might use soft, warm pastels, whereas excitement might be expressed with garish primaries or neon colors. Nostalgia would call for glowing, sepia tones. Study the colors around you for their emotional messages. Movie posters, magazine ads, or paintings in a museum are all good subjects for evaluating the effect of color on mood.

How would you change the palette of Kenneth Branagh's *Hamlet* poster if the movie was a comedy, for example? Or how would you alter the palette and mood of the poster if Darth Vader was the hero of *The Empire Strikes Back*, which chronicled the Empire's valiant attempts to fend off a crazed band of rebels?

Some artists add colors that are unexpected or unrealistic to a painting to intensify its emotional content. The luminous glows seen in Renoir's paintings of nudes are not really present in the human form, but he must have seen them on some level as he painted the vision in his mind's eye. Don't be afraid to use colors in your work that impart a personal style.

Surveying some sample palettes

To see the relationship of palette and atmosphere, study the following palette examples and the descriptions of their associated images. Notice the color atmosphere of each and compare and contrast them to one another. See how the colors of trees in the spring differ from those of trees in the fall and how a city scene changes color from day to night. (If you want to use any of these palettes for your own work, they can all be found at the *Fine Art Photoshop* web site, **www.digitalsketch.com**.)

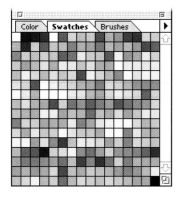

(photo by Flo Scott)

Figure II.A.1
The Delaware picnic photo here is the basis for Palette 1, above.

Palette 1—This palette and its image pair (see Figure II.A.1) contain a profusion of different blues (the water and the sky) and very subtle, understated greens (the bright, sunlit grassy areas and their deep shadows). The palette is notable for its lack of any warm colors except for a few bright blues. The atmosphere of this palette combines the warmth of the sunny day with a feeling of cool breezes blowing in off the ocean. Although not many different hues are used, just look at the range of expression such a limited palette can yield.

Palette 2—This palette is taken from the picture of an English pond in the winter. The warm brownish greens and soft yellows are muted and subtle. The darker colors suggest shadows and depth. You can almost hear the frogs croaking and see the weak winter sun casting a warm glow on the murky water. The light browns could be from the mud around the bank. The palette has great atmosphere.

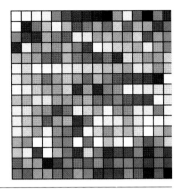

Palette 3—In this palette, you see the streets of a European city on a rainy day. Rain creates a particularly romantic atmosphere as the puddles reflect light and color. Look how many shades of gray it takes to describe sidewalks, asphalt, and buildings. Is the dark red color from a passing car or an umbrella? Perhaps the multitude of light brown colors are from an awning over a shuttered sidewalk cafe.

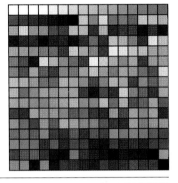

Palette 4—This palette is comprised mostly of different hues of the primary colors red, blue, and yellow. A Mediterranean village is the source for these colors. It's not difficult to imagine the red and pink tile roofs, ochre buildings, blue sky and sea, or the gray greens of grape leaves. The preponderance of shadow suggests late afternoon.

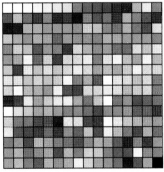

Palette 5—The colors in this palette are a series of green and gray hues in a range of values from light to dark. This is the palette from a piece of green marble. You can easily see how these colors might be played out in the streaks found in a beautiful piece of stone. Maybe it's now on the lobby walls of a nearby branch bank.

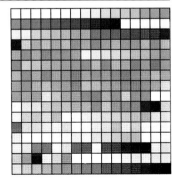

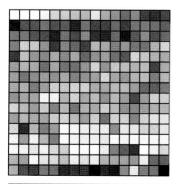

Palette 6—This palette is taken from a picture of people around a campfire. Look closely and you can see their glowing faces painted in the hues of the yellows and oranges, the brown colors of the wood they're burning, its white-hot coals and gray ashes. Watch the red sparks rise into the sky. Look at the blacks and dark grays of the shadows and the forest surrounding them.

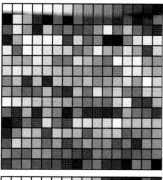

The two palettes shown here are from the same urban scene, at different times of day. The first is seen in brilliant sunshine, the second on a foggy night.

Palette 7—Brightly painted San Francisco Victorians stand in the foreground; the downtown skyline towers behind with a glimpse of the Bay. The blues suggest the sky and its reflection in the windows of the buildings.

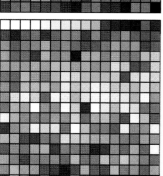

Palette 8—Same Victorians, same view point, different time of day. The yellow glow of lights from the skyscrapers in the distance blends into a foggy night sky. Streetlights cast a greenish aura onto the front of the houses.

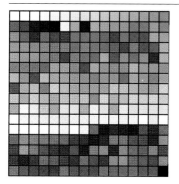

Palette 9—Here you see the colors from a picture of sunset on a beach. The sky almost seems to be on fire, and as the sun sinks in the horizon, its colors are reflected in the water. There is not a great range in hues here: Note the complete lack of blues and greens, but what a riot of red, orange, and yellow!

These two palettes are both from pictures of the Southwest. Compare them and get a feel for how the colors in each tell a different story.

Palette 10—The cool blues and browns of this palette are derived from an image of buttes in the Southwest. The violet colors suggest the twilight, a rising moon, and the deepening shadows, whereas the reds are the glow of the setting sun on the rocky landscape.

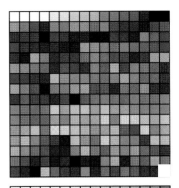

Palette 11—This set of colors also originates in the Southwest: a town in New Mexico. The colors come from adobe buildings, warm sunshine, and cool shadows under arcades. The muted greens could be the colors of cacti and other succulents growing around the town square.

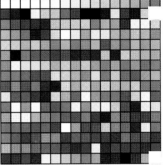

Fall scenes are favorite subjects for many artists because of their rich colors and play of light. Compare these two palettes, both from forest scenes in autumn.

Palette 12—A stand of maples in the fall displays the rich reds and oranges you would expect in this palette, but what's the source of all the pink? This is an example of how light affects color. It falls, dappled and filtered, through the red leaves, making some of the leaves appear pink.

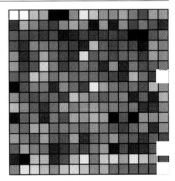

Palette 13—Judging from all the yellows in this palette, the trees are probably aspens or poplars, with a warm afternoon sun lighting them. You can almost hear the crisp crunch of leaves underfoot on this dry, autumn day.

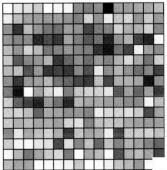

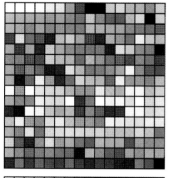

All four palettes here are taken from woodland scenes in different parts of the US. Notice the similarities and differences they all display.

Palette 14—A New England forest with a brook running through it is the source of these colors. It contains a lively variety of greens and blues. This palette suggests the lushness of dense forest growth and humidity of a summer day, and the blue water promises cooling refreshment.

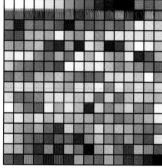

Palette 15—The bright yellows and yellow greens in this palette bring to mind daffodils, ferns, and the vibrancy of a spring morning in this forest scene, somewhere in the Midwest. The reds could be from a barn, or maybe wildflowers in the foreground.

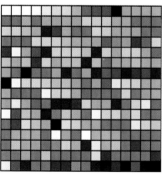

Palette 16—The greens in this palette are from a woods in the deep South, in the heat of summer. They show an intricate interplay of light and shadow in an otherwise monochromatic composition. Notice how much warmer these greens appear than those from the New England forest scene.

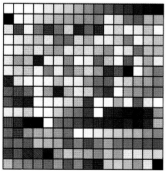

Palette 17—Would you have guessed that these colors are also from trees, in this case, Yosemite pines in winter? The needles on the trees exhibit a blue cast, and you can feel the fading twilight, with its cool shadows in this exquisite palette.

Color modes in Photoshop

When you paint in Photoshop, it's best to work in RGB mode. This is the native mode your monitor uses to display colors, making it a more efficient way to work with and save files. Additionally, many of Photoshop's filters work only in RGB. Depending on your painting's eventual output requirements, you can change the mode later.

RGB monitors can display many more colors than the traditional cyan/magenta/yellow/black printing process can reproduce with only four colors of ink. This means that it's possible for you to choose onscreen colors that will not print accurately later. Photoshop solves this problem for you by identifying these nonprintable colors with a triangle on the Color Picker. Double-click the Foreground color to open the Color Picker. If you see the triangle displayed, click it, and the foreground color changes to the closest approximation that can be printed in CMYK (see Figure II.A.2).

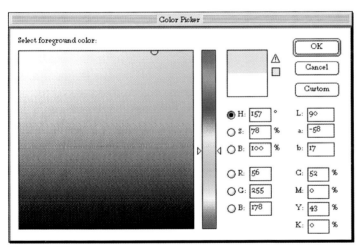

Figure II.A.2
The color being used can't be printed in CMYK if the triangle appears on the Color Picker.

Building custom palettes in Photoshop

When you set out to build a custom palette in Photoshop, you can approach the task in three ways. You can load the existing palette from the scan of a photo, build up a series of swatches by choosing individual colors, or mix colors at random in a scratch file and add them when you find ones you like. Each method has its own advantages and disadvantages, and each is described here.

Taking a palette from an existing image

Borrowing a palette from an existing Photoshop image is quick and easy. When you use this method to create a custom palette, you have the advantage of a wide range of colors you might otherwise not think of adding. This method, however, limits you to colors someone else has already chosen.

Open an existing Photoshop file and follow these steps:

1. Be sure the file is in RGB mode. Then convert from RGB to Indexed color by selecting **Image➡Mode➡Indexed Color**. Use Adaptive, 256 colors, no dithering settings.

2. Select **Image➡Mode➡Color Table**.

3. When the Color Table dialog box opens, choose **Save**.

4. Name the file and place the saved table in the Photoshop Color Palettes folder.

5. From the Swatches palette, click the arrow in the upper-right corner and scroll down to select **Replace Swatches**.

After you create a new palette this way, save it by choosing **Save Swatches** from the Swatches palette. Name the new palette and save it in the Photoshop Goodies folder (Macintosh) or Palettes folder (Windows). Now you can use the newly created color palette on any future file simply by opening a new file and loading the table from the Swatches palette.

Building a palette using the Trumatch color system

Whether your image is going to be printed in vast quantities with the traditional offset method or be produced in limited numbers on an IRIS or other color printer, it's important that the colors you use on-screen print accurately in the CMYK mode. CMYK stands for Cyan, Magenta, Yellow, and Black, the four colors of ink that are combined to produce a wide range of printed colors.

Use the Trumatch color system to build a palette when your painting is destined for printing with the CMYK process. This ensures that any color you choose prints correctly.

1. Click the foreground color to open the Color Picker (see Figure II.A.2).

2. Choose **Custom** on the Color Picker to open the Custom Color palette (see Figure II.A.3).

3. Scroll through the Book pull-down menu to Trumatch (see Figure II.A.4). When you want to add a color to the Swatches palette, select it and click OK. The color you selected becomes the new foreground color. Move your cursor over the Swatches palette to the first empty space. Your cursor changes to a paint bucket, and when you click, the color is added to the palette.

4. Repeat step 3 to add more colors.

5. Remove unwanted colors from the palette by pressing the **Command** key (Macintosh) or **Ctrl** key (Windows) to change the cursor to a small scissors and click the color you want to remove.

6. After filling your palette with a full range of colors, choose **Save Swatches** from the Swatches palette, name and save the new palette in the Photoshop Goodies folder (Macintosh) or Palettes folder (Windows).

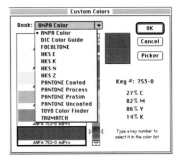

Figure II.A.3
The Custom Color palette opens when you choose Custom on the Color Picker.

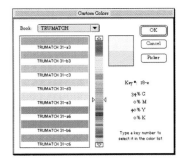

Figure II.A.4
Custom Color palette set to Trumatch system in a range of aqua blues.

Building a palette using a scratch file

This method of building a palette using a scratch file approximates that used by a traditional artist mixing colors from tubes of paint. The advantage of building a palette this way lies in the surprises you get when unexpected colors result from the mixing process. A possible disadvantage is that you may create some colors that look great on-screen but do not print accurately.

1. Open a new Photoshop file in RGB mode.

2. Click the Foreground color to open the Color Picker.

3. Choose any color you want in the Color Picker by clicking it. That color becomes the Foreground color.

4. Press **B** to change to the Paintbrush. Select a large brush and paint a stroke of the color on your canvas.

5. Randomly choose other colors for the Foreground color, and with the Paintbrush Opacity set at a level lower than 50%, paint strokes of the new colors across the original stroke. This results in blended colors where the strokes overlap and mix together.

6. Change to the Eyedropper tool by pressing **I** and click down in any area that contains a color you want to add to the palette. Move your cursor over the Swatches palette and click in a blank space to add the new color. Continue until you have built up a palette you want to use.

7. When you're finished, save the palette in the Photoshop Goodies folder (Macintosh) or Palettes folder (Windows). You can delete the scratch file or save it for developing more colors later on.

Using your palette efficiently

After you've built a palette for your work, it can be kept open and moved next to the area of the image you're painting. When you drag your brush onto the palette, the cursor immediately changes to the Eyedropper tool so that you can easily switch to a new color. Then when you move the cursor back to where you were working, it becomes the brush again.

In the following lessons, you build palettes appropriate for the atmosphere, lighting conditions, and emotional content you want to bring to your paintings. Don't think of these palettes—or any palettes—as static. You can always add colors whether they're the result of a happy blending accident, different lighting conditions, or a change in your mood.

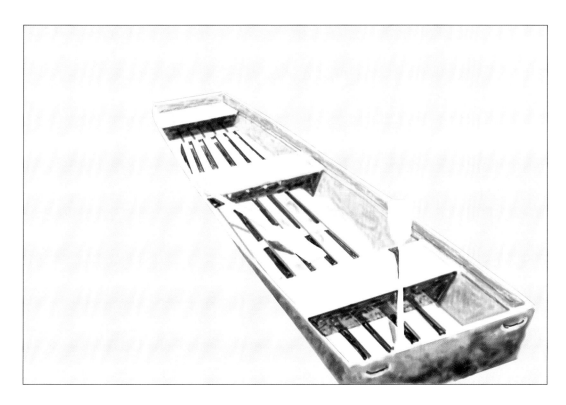

Part II: Lesson B **Painting in watercolor style**

In this lesson, you become a digital watercolorist, applying color and atmosphere to your boat sketch. The basic steps are: open Part I, Lesson A's pencil drawing; add a new layer, which can be used to hide the pencil drawing; add a third layer; and paint in Photoshop to achieve a watercolor effect.

The atmospheric and emotional effects you want to achieve determine the colors you choose for a palette. The light and dark values in your original drawing help you select which

Art concepts

Light

Shadow

Contrast

Value

Color combinations

Tonality

Transparency and blending

Photoshop tools and features

Paintbrush

Color palettes

Layers

Paths

Pen tool

Focusing tools

Toning tools

Smudge tool

colors to paint in which areas. You can choose the colors of an aluminum boat sitting in the sun—various hues of gray. The shadowed areas under the seats call for dark gray-browns, and the weathered wood floorboards can be suggested by bleached-out grays and light browns. The oars could be a yellowish color.

You discover how to blend colors and alter their transparency as you work with different size brushes. Larger brushes are used to paint sections of the boat's sides, and smaller ones to make the shadows cast by the boat's floorboards.

Change to RGB mode

Open your original working file for the boat drawing and choose **Save As**, naming the new file *Boat 2*. Your palette is displayed in grayscale. Choose **Image➥Mode➥RGB Color**. Your palette defaults back to color, and you're ready to select your color combinations.

Choose an atmosphere for your landscape

Study the reference photograph again and decide on your boat's location, the time of day, and other atmosphere issues. Perhaps it's a winter day with rain falling on the pond. Or, maybe the boat sits on a Caribbean beach at sunrise. Use your imagination.

Create a custom color palette

Because the boat drawing in Part I, Lesson A is realistic, this lesson's examples use a realistic palette. The dark greens reflected in the water are from the trees surrounding the pond, somewhere in North America on a June day. It's about two o'clock in the afternoon; with a clear, blue summer sky. The boat is aluminum, its surface roughened by many years of weathering, its color bleached by the sun.

Follow the steps for building a custom palette with the Trumatch system from Part II, Lesson A, adding the atmospheric and emotional colors you want to use for your painting. Scroll through the Trumatch choices and add every dark green you envision in the water or every light blue that might be good for the reflection of the sky. You need some light browns for the wood, footprints, and oars, as well as some colors for the sand. Add a complete range of grays—warm, cool, and neutral—from the lightest ones to the darkest. The Trumatch palette groups the grays at the bottom of the color strip. Finally, add some vibrant, moody, or discordant colors that you can use to heighten the emotional content of your painting. For instance, if you're trying to achieve a festive scene, some reds and yellows would be an unexpected addition of color. Or, if you want a tranquil mood, violets or deep purples might be appropriate.

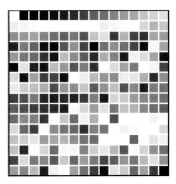

Figure II.B.1
The custom palette created by the authors to paint the boat.

With your palette ready, choose Save Swatches from the Swatches palette. (Figure II.B.1 shows the example palette.) Name it *Boat/Pond* and save it to the Color Palettes folder inside Photoshop's Goodies folder (Macintosh) or Palettes Folder (Windows). Each time you save the palette after adding or deleting colors, you have to re-enter the name and replace the previous file. If you want more than 256 colors for your painting, create a second new palette and save it as *Boat/Pond2*. Load it also into the Swatches palette.

Make a new layer to obscure the boat drawing

For this exercise, you need a layer that can be turned off and on to hide the drawing below it. Select **Layer➥New** and name the layer *Paper*. Make the foreground color a light gray (R 210, G 210, B 210). From the menu bar, choose **Select➥All**; then press **Option-Delete** (Macintosh) or **Alt-Backspace** (Windows) to fill the layer with white. The boat image is hidden from view by the Paper layer. When you hide the Paper layer, you can use the drawing you did of the boat to guide your paintbrush strokes. Then when you show the Paper layer again, you can isolate your new brush strokes from the outline and crosshatching below the Paper layer. For now, hide the Paper layer by clicking its Eye icon in the Layers palette.

Make a new layer for painting

Now add another layer that you can use to paint the boat and name it *Paint*. When you make the Paper layer invisible, you can use the drawing you did of the boat to guide your paintbrush strokes. Then when you make the Paper layer visible again, you can isolate your brush strokes from the outline and crosshatching below the Paper layer. The experience of painting on the gray background simulates using a dark watercolor paper and helps you learn to paint with lighter colors and white.

Begin painting the inside of the boat

You begin with the inside of the boat for a couple of reasons. First, the inside represents the focal point of the picture. In the original reference photograph in Part I, Lesson A, you can see wet footprints on the floorboards, which tell a story: only moments ago, a child rowed this boat to shore and got out.

Second, the inside of the boat contains large areas of unbroken color, as well as smaller, more confined areas. Starting inside gives you a chance to get familiar with easier brush strokes before moving on to more difficult ones.

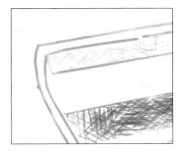

Figure II.B.2
Display the pencil sketch of the boat drawing to guide your first brush strokes.

Paint the front seat

Begin with the Paper layer hidden. If you are painting the boat in realistic colors, choose a very light gray from your color palette. (If you are painting with a different color combination, choose another very light color.) Choose the Paintbrush by pressing **B**. Set the brush to 50% transparency and select a medium large, soft-edged brush tip. Make short overlapping strokes in the front seat. Show the Paper layer and see how your strokes are building up. Paint a few strokes with the pencil sketch hidden. Don't worry about paint spilling beyond the edges of the seat; that will be easy to correct later. Hide the Paper layer again.

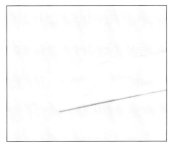

Figure II.B.3
Hide the sketch to evaluate the strokes.

Remember to keep the Color Swatch palette open and near the area you're painting; dragging the cursor over the palette changes the cursor to the Eyedropper so that you can change paint colors easily.

Next, choose another, slightly different hue of your light color and make some new strokes blending into the first ones. Repeat the process until you have blended the two colors to your satisfaction. You can add a third light hue, but always keep your brush semitransparent so that your brush strokes blend.

Change the color to white and paint in some strokes. When you can no longer see the crosshatching from the drawing underneath the paint, you have probably applied enough paint (see Figure II.B.2 and Figure II.B.3).

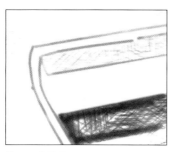

Figure II.B.4
Use Shift to make linear brush strokes.

Figure II.B.5
Light and dark colors are used to paint the front of the boat, the seat, and the shadow underneath the seat.

Figure II.B.6
The inside wall of the boat is painted using a series of blue-gray colors.

Paint the front of the boat

The front of the boat is in shadow and is a darker gray than the seat. Because it's smaller and more confined, you can paint it better with a smaller brush tip.

Remember, you can easily cycle through the brush tips by pressing **[** or **]** (left or right bracket key). Change the opacity of a tool in 10% increments by pressing number keys **1,2,3,...9,0**.

Keep your opacity below 50%, choose several medium gray colors, and paint the area as you did the seat. To outline the area, hold down the **Shift** key, click on the top-left corner, move to the top-right corner, and click again. Change colors and lengths of the stroke as you outline the entire area so that the strokes do not become too built up and obvious. They should blend with the strokes you use to fill the interior area (see Figure II.B.4).

Paint the shadow beneath the seat

Now switch to the dark grays, browns, and blacks in your palette and fill in the shadow area beneath the seat. Don't be concerned about getting the paint too dark; with digital watercolor, you can go back and lighten to establish detail in a way you cannot with the traditional watercolor medium (see Figure II.B.5).

Paint the inside wall of the boat

The inside wall of the boat is a bluish hue of the medium gray. Begin filling it in, again using a series of colors with similar values and different hues and semitransparent brush strokes. Keep viewing your painting with the Paper layer turned on and off, and work strokes in both views (see Figure II.B.6).

Paint the floorboards

Start with very light tans and warm grays and color in the light areas of the floorboards. Add some strokes in white to lighten the colors.

To define the edges of the floorboards, change your foreground color to a dark brown and use **Shift** to make straight strokes. Finally, switch to the darkest browns, grays, and black to fill in the shadow areas (see Figure II.B.7).

Paint the remaining seats and floorboards

As you become familiar with the techniques for painting the seats, shadows, and floorboards, move towards the back of the boat. Leave the oars unpainted for the time being.

Paint the outside edge of the boat

Using a small brush with opacity set to 80% or more, paint a heavy white outline for the top edge of the boat. If you find it difficult to keep the edge straight, you might want to use the Pen tool to define a path first and then stroke it. If you use this method, make several short strokes rather than one sweeping, long stroke to avoid making the painting look too mechanical. Change to a very light gray or blue gray and paint in some strokes with a more transparent setting of 30% or less to blend some other colors into the edge of the boat.

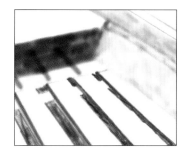

Figure II.B.7
Light tans and grays combine with darker browns, grays, and black to paint the boat's floorboards.

Figure II.B.8
Outline the oars with the Pen tool, make the selection active, and fill with white.

Paint the oars

In the original photograph, the oars appear almost white and almost completely flat. Because they are such a focal point of the painting, the oars should stand out. An easy way to accomplish this is to use the Pen tool to outline each oar, select the oar, and fill it with 100% white or very light gray. Here's how it's done:

1. Select the Pen tool and click at the top-left corner of the oar on the right. Click again in the same location to drag out a short handle, move across the top of the oar, and click at the top, right corner. Drag out another short handle and continue your way around the complete oar.

2. When you reach your starting point, click to complete the outline of the oar.

3. Hold down the **Command** key (Macintosh) or **Ctrl** key (Windows) to change the Pen tool to the Direct Selection tool. Adjust the outline of the oar to make it more accurate by clicking and moving the points, handles, or lines. When satisfied with the outline, choose **Make Selection** from the Paths palette. To save the path for use later, choose **Select➥Save Selection**.

4. Select white or very light gray as the foreground color. Choose **Edit➥Fill** and, when the dialog box appears, make sure that the Opacity is 100% and Mode is Normal. Click **OK**, and the oar is filled with the light color; no other colors show through.

5. Click the trash can in the lower right-hand corner of the Paths palette to remove the path outline.

6. While the oar is still selected, choose some slightly darker color variations and with a very small brush, at 50% or less opacity, paint some strokes to blend into the filled area to create shadow and depth in the oar (see Figure II.B.8).

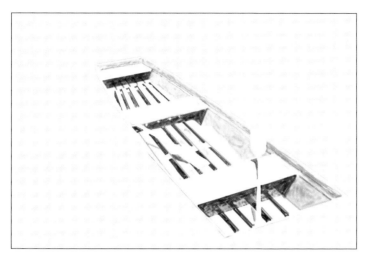

Figure II.B.9
Add outlines and other details; then use the Blur tool to soften them.

Add final outline and detail

Now you can carefully add lines to outline the boat and create other definition. An efficient way to do this is to switch to the Pen tool by pressing **P** and create your outline with several curved lines that you can later stroke. Before clicking the Stroke icon in the Paths palette (the circle second from the left), change your paint color to a medium–dark gray, choose a small brush tip, and set the transparency level at 50% or below so that these lines are subtle. If they look too uniform or hard edged, you might want to switch to the Focus tools by pressing **R** and drag the Blur tool over the lines until they are softer (see Figure II.B.9).

Paint the outside of the boat

As you paint the outside of the boat, it is helpful to select just the area you're working on to avoid the darker colors spilling into the inside. Select the Pen tool again and click at the top-left corner. Click again in the same location to drag out a short handle, move across the back of the boat, and click at the top–right corner. Continue to outline the area you want to paint and, after you click your starting point to complete the polygon, choose **Make Selection** from the Paths palette menu. The area you've outlined becomes active, and paint does not spill outside its borders (see Figure II.B.10).

Figure II.B.10
Use the Pen tool to outline the back of the boat with the template showing and make the selection active.

Use a series of colors in a dark gray range and a large, soft-edged, semitransparent brush with pixel width of 65. Switch among the various hues and blend strokes to fill in the dark back of the boat. Change to a light gray or white color and, using a very small brush, paint in the handles. Switch to black and paint shadows for the handles.

After you finish the back of the boat, use the Pen tool to select the small outside portion seen on the left side and paint it with the same kind of strokes and colors you used for the back.

Paint in the wet feet on the floorboards

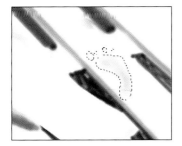

Figure II.B.11
Create outlines of the footprints with the Lasso tool and fill them with a darker brown.

Choose the Lasso tool by pressing **L** and check Anti-aliased in the Lasso Options palette. Zoom in to a high level of magnification and use the Lasso to draw the outline of a footprint. Hold down **Shift** and draw some toes. Switch to a light brown foreground color and select **Edit➡Fill**. Specify an opacity of 10% and fill the foot. If it doesn't look dark enough, you can fill it a second or third time. A transparent fill made this way simulates the look of wet footprints because it allows the texture of the wood to show through the transparency, just as it would in real life. Repeat drawing one or two other footprints and some additional water spills and use the same fill level to color them (see Figure II.B.11).

Blend rough areas with the Smudge tool

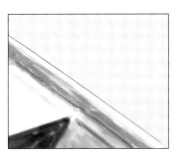

Figure II.B.12
The Smudge tool can be used to blend rough edges.

Take a look at your painting with the pencil drawing hidden, Paper layer showing. You can use the Smudge tool to blend areas that look too rough. Use a large, soft-edged brush at 50% opacity or less and gradually smudge the rough area so that you don't lose the effect of the blended brushstrokes (see Figure II.B.12).

Darken/lighten areas with the Toning tools

Do a final touch-up of your painting by using the Toning tools to dodge (lighten) or burn (darken) areas. Press **O** to change to the Toning tool and press **O** again to cycle through the Dodge, Burn, and Sponge tools. Because the Dodge and Burn tools can have a heavy impact on your painting, set the Pressure level to 50% or below. Use Dodge to lighten areas such as the seat tops and Burn to darken areas such as the shadows under the seats. Choose a brush the right size for the area you want to affect— small and focused for small areas, such as the shadows between the floorboards, and larger for areas such as the sides of the boat.

This completes the first lesson in watercolor. Save your working file and keep it for Part III, Lesson A, where you use a wash to paint the water and complete the painting.

If you want to print this image using the four-color process, choose **Layer➡Flatten Image** and then **Save As** (with a different file name) to make another in the TIFF format.

Part II: Lesson C   ## Coloring the self-portrait in "pastels"

By coloring the charcoal-effect drawing from Part I, Lesson B, you can add new dimension and mood to your self-portrait. Color conveys messages on many levels; use it to realistically portray your subject or to add atmosphere and mood. In this lesson, you learn how to create a palette with a wide range of skin tones and other colors and then how to apply them in a manner that looks like a traditional pastel portrait.

The wide range of colors that make up different people's complexions are further affected

Art concepts

Light

Shadow

Contrast

Value

Color combinations

Tonality

Transparency and blending

Skin tones

Photoshop tools and features

Airbrush

Color palettes

Layers

Paths

Focusing tools

Toning tools

Smudge tool

by lighting conditions, contrast with backgrounds and clothing colors, and the emotional content brought to a painting by the artist.

When working in the traditional pastel medium, the artist blends and smudges colors laid down by the dusty crayons and builds up areas of color layer by layer. The final result is sprayed with a fixative to keep the color from being brushed off. Photoshop is particularly well-suited for creating a pastel look, and the digital method is much more forgiving and much less messy.

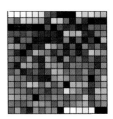

Prepare the portrait and change Mode

Open your original working file for the self-portrait, choose **Save As**, and give the file a new name. At first, your palette will appear in grayscale. Choose **Image➡Mode➡RGB Color**, and the palette will default back to color. Now you're ready to select your color combinations.

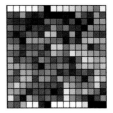

Choose an atmosphere

You can color your charcoal drawing using the actual colors you see in the mirror, or you can use your imagination to change the conditions and atmosphere. For instance, if you did your original sketch using artificial light, you can create the pastel drawing to suggest daylight. Maybe you'll place yourself outdoors, or in a dimly lit room. Whatever conditions and atmosphere you choose for your portrait will affect the colors in the palette.

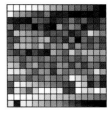

Study some sample skin-tone palettes

Figures II.C.1 to II.C.6 show a number of custom palettes that represent different skin tones for people of various ethnic and racial backgrounds. They cover the color spectrum of human-kind—from an African princess to a young Shanghai mother, a Hispanic grandfather, and a platinum blond Swedish baby. Perhaps the most striking thing about these palettes is not how different they are but rather their similarity. Study these palettes, and you'll see eye and hair colors as well as skin tones.

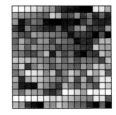

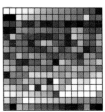

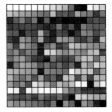

Figures II.C.1 to II.C.6
A sampling of the 30 skin-tone palettes representing people around the world that are available at the Fine Art Photoshop web site (**www.digitalsketch.com**).

Figure II.C.7
Use the basic colors of your skin and overlapping Airbrush strokes to create a variety of hues for your palette.

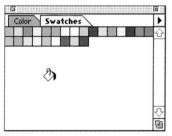

Figure II.C.8
Here is the custom palette used to color the example shown.

Create a custom palette

The lesson's example portrait assumes that the subject is seen in very bright lighting conditions. The predominant colors used to create it are pink and yellow. Other combinations for suggesting skin tone might use browns and reds, and of course, there's always the olive-toned complexion. By laying down strokes of various color tones and blending them, you can create a wide range of colors to build an appropriate palette for a portrait.

Press **A** to choose the Airbrush tool; then press **Return** (Macintosh) or **Enter** (Windows) to open the Airbrush Options palette. Set Opacity at 80%, select Wet Edges to allow for colors to blend to a greater degree, and choose Normal for the mode. Open the Brushes palette, and select the 100-pixel diameter, soft-edged brush.

Make a new layer and name it *Base*. Click the foreground color box on the Photoshop toolbox, and when the Color Picker appears, choose a base color for your skin tone. (The subject in Figure II.C.7 starts in the pink range.) Make some broad strokes on the *Base* layer. Switch foreground color to yellow or brown, depending on the tonal blends you want, and make strokes that blend into the first one. Keep changing colors and adding strokes until you have a wide range from which to choose.

Follow the steps for building a custom palette from a Scratch file from Part II, Lesson A, and use the Eyedropper tool to add colors to your palette. Add every color that might be used in suggesting your range of skin tones as seen in light and shadow. You'll need additional colors for your hair, eyes, clothing, and background elements.

With your palette ready, choose **Save Swatches** from the Swatches palette menu. Name it *Portrait*, and save it to the Color Palettes folder inside Photoshop's Goodies folder (Macintosh) or Palettes folder (Windows). Each time you save the palette after adding or deleting colors, you must re-enter the name and replace the previous file. The palette for the portrait we are using is shown in Figure II.C.8.

Hide the charcoal drawing

After you build your palette, make the foreground color white (R255, G255, B255). Select everything on the Base layer by pressing **Command-A** (Macintosh) or **Ctrl-A** (Windows); then press **Option-Delete** (Macintosh) or **Alt-Backspace** (Windows) to fill the layer with white. The charcoal drawing is hidden from view by the Base layer. When you hide the Base layer, you can use your charcoal drawing to guide your paintbrush strokes. Then when you show the Base layer again, you can view your new brush strokes separate from the drawing below.

For now, hide the Base layer by clicking its Eye icon in the Layers palette.

Begin painting on a new layer

Now add another layer, which you will use to paint your portrait, and name it *Pastels*. Switch to the Paintbrush by pressing **B**, and on the Paintbrush Options palette, make Opacity 100% and set Fade to Transparent at 10 steps. Select Wet Edges by clicking in the box at the bottom of the Options palette.

Choose a soft-edged brush tip of about 45 pixels in diameter. Change the foreground color to a dark version of your basic skin tone, and begin laying down a base color over the areas of darkest shadow.

Adjust the number of Fade steps and the Opacity level liberally as you stroke around the face. Some areas need a short shadow, others long. For example, depending on the light source, there might be shorter shadows at the top of your nose than at the bottom.

Next, block in your hair with a middle color value and a 100-pixel, soft-edged brush. Follow with main areas of color in your clothing. Figure II.C.9 shows the first color strokes with the charcoal layer in view; Figure II.C.10 shows the same strokes with the charcoal layer hidden.

Figure II.C.9
The first brush strokes with the charcoal layer visible.

Figure II.C.10
The same brush strokes with the charcoal layer hidden.

Figure II.C.11
Add highlights on the face and shadows in the hair.

Add more color and detail

Next, add the brighter highlights to your face and add shadows to your hair. Creating the appearance of hair is very complex and needs the darkest areas blocked in first so that you can go back later to add very bright strokes over the top. Begin with large brushes to block in areas of darker, underlying colors, and go over them with progressively smaller, lighter brush strokes. Then go back in and add some small, dark strokes for detail.

Change the brush tip size, color, opacity level, and number of fade steps of your strokes to create more variety (see Figure II.C.11).

Add detail lines for features and shadows

Switch to a small brush tip and turn off Wet Edges. Enhance each shadow by laying a darker edge on its perimeter. Then add a lighter highlight outside the shadow to show the crest of the facial feature or wrinkle.

Add detail strokes with a very small brush and a dark color; use the Eraser tool to clean up outside edges (see Figure II.C.12).

Figure II.C.12
Add dark, fine lines to define shadows and facial features.

Blend the colors

Switch to the Smudge tool by pressing **U**. On the Smudge Tool Options palette, set Pressure at 30% and choose a soft-edged brush tip, 9 pixels in diameter (second from the left on the second row).

Take the Smudge tool to your painting and move the color around to blend it much the same as you'd do with your finger or a paper stump if you were working with real pastels. Notice that when you begin smudging in one color, it extends outward over the adjacent color. Smudge in opposite directions to smooth colors so that you don't end up just pushing one color into the other. Be sure to smudge the dark lines you drew for detail around the facial features and near shadows; you may want to use a smaller brush tip for this purpose.

Continue to lay in color and then smudge it to build up the effect of a pastel drawing (see Figure II.C.13).

Figure II.C.13
Smudge to blend colors just as you would if working in the traditional pastel medium.

Add a color wash to unify the composition

Sometimes the colors in a composition can be too different from each other, and make a jarring, rather than unified, effect. If this is the case with your work so far, you can add a light color wash to unify it (something not possible with traditional pastels). Create another new layer, and switch to the Lasso tool by pressing **L**. Loosely surround the face and neck with the Lasso to select only the areas of skin. Hold the **Option** key (Macintosh) or **Alt** key (Windows), and lasso the eyes and mouth so they are subtracted from the selection. Choose **Select➥Feather** and when the dialog box appears, set a Feather radius of 6 to 8 pixels. Click **OK**. This will prevent a harsh color transition at the edge when you fill the selection with color.

Make the foreground color your basic skin tone, and select **Edit➥Fill**. When the dialog box opens, set Opacity at 20% and Mode to Multiply. When you click **OK**, the light wash of skin tone will fill the selected area and unify its color, and the Multiply mode will help retain the detail.

Similarly, select the hair with the Lasso tool and fill it with a light wash of its basic color. Do the same with the clothing (see Figure II.C.14). Finally, lower the Opacity level of the layer so that the wash isn't too strong.

Figure II.C.14
A light wash over each of the primary areas of color will unify the composition and make the form appear more solid.

Figure II.C.15
The Rough Pastels filter can add the look of texture from rough paper and the dust of real pastels.

Use the Rough Pastels Artistic Filter

Now, you can add a final touch that will make your composition seem like it was created with real pastel crayons on rough paper. But before you apply the Rough Pastels filter, you may want to save a copy of your work at this stage. This is because the global application of this—or any—filter will alter your carefully laid down strokes and may change your work in ways you don't like.

Make the original charcoal drawing layer invisible (if desired), and merge all layers by selecting **Layer➡Flatten Image**. Then choose **Filter➡Artistic➡Rough Pastels**. When the Rough Pastels dialog box opens, adjust the options for Stroke Length and Detail (the example here used 10 for Stroke Length and 5 for Detail). You can choose from four textures by using the pull-down menu, (Sandstone was used here) and set the Scaling, Relief, and Light Direction variables. The settings you choose will apply to the sample area on the palette, though you may have to wait a moment for changes to take effect. When you're satisfied with the settings, click **OK** to apply the filter, as seen in Figure II.C.15.

Now that you've seen how easy it is to create a pastel version of your self-portrait, you may want to try the techniques with other subjects. Pastels lend themselves well to coloring landscapes, still lifes, and portraits.

To output your self-portrait at this stage, save a copy as a CMYK TIFF. Keep a working copy, as well. You'll use it later in Part III for creating an oil-painted effect and in Part IV for a "resist" technique.

Part II: Lesson D   Adding color to the still life

In this lesson, you add color and emotion to the drawing of lemons you created in Part I. First, you make a custom palette containing yellows and yellow-greens in different color tones to indicate the natural appearance of the lemons, as well as a several hues of dark grays and violets to describe the shadows they cast. Violet is yellow's complementary—or opposite—color.

The palette also should include some colors for emotional content, such as reds, oranges, bright

Art concepts

Hue

Saturation

Complementary color

Emotional color

Warm and cool colors

Simultaneous contrast

Depth of field

Volume

Photoshop tools and features

Layers

Masks

Airbrush

Lasso

Hue/Saturation settings

blues, and greens. These colors add emotional content because they are not "expected" when viewing lemons on a white background. Instead, emotional colors are drawn from the artist's imagination and can be used to suggest a variety of feelings, from warmth and joy to darkness and despair. In this example, the emotional colors are used sparingly, primarily in the shadows, and suggest a cool, detached feeling.

Rather than painting over the black-and-white version of the lemons, you learn how to colorize the existing airbrush strokes in the painting, building on the texture and blended shading you created in the original version. By loading the selections made in the Part I lesson, you isolate portions of the painting and add color to them by changing hue and saturation. Finally, you use the Airbrush tool to color specific pixels.

Prepare the lemons painting

After opening the Part I drawing, choose **Image➥Mode➥RGB Color**. When you change Mode, a prompt appears asking whether you want to flatten layers. Click Flatten because this results in a smaller file size. Then select **File➥Save As** and give the new file a different name from the original.

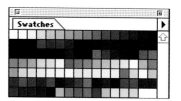

Figure II.D.1
The authors' custom palette for the lemons painting.

Build a custom palette

If you still have the composition set up next to your computer, take a good look at the range of colors in the lemons and the shadows cast by them onto the paper. Create a palette with as many of these colors as possible and add others for emotional content and visual interest. Although all you will be painting are the lemons, you still want to suggest more than what the viewer can see. Create an air of mystery to keep the viewer interested and looking for more in your painting.

If you study, for example, Impressionist and Post-Impressionist still lifes, you will find unexpected, often discordant colors. These colors were added to create visual interest in simple compositions or subjects. Discordance plays a role by becoming a placemarker to attract and draw the viewer's eye into the composition. Figure II.D.1 shows the custom palette created for this painting; it is available at the *Fine Art Photoshop* web site, **www.digitalsketch.com**.

To build your own custom palette, refer to Part II, Lesson A, and follow the instructions for building a palette using the Trumatch color system.

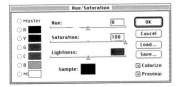

Figure II.D.2
The Hue/Saturation palette can be used to colorize black-and-white images.

Colorize the lemon selections

The selections you saved when creating the original black-and-white painting should still be available. Load these selections, so you can change the black-and-white shading and texture of the lemons to a dark yellow-orange.

1. Choose **Select➥Load Selection** and pick the first lemon. Load the other two lemons one by one by choosing **Add to Selection** on the Load Selection palette. If you want, you can choose **Save Selection** to group all three lemons to make working with them easier.

2. Choose **Image➥Adjust➥Hue/Saturation**. When the Hue/Saturation palette opens (see Figure II.D.2), click the Colorize box on the bottom right. Be sure Preview is also checked. The lemons will probably turn red.

3. Move the Hue slider until the lemons have changed to a yellow-orange color. The numerical setting for this hue is between 40 and 50, with 40 being more orange, 50 more yellow. The colors seen here show a Hue setting of 45. Note how darker parts of the original lemons are now dark yellow, with lighter areas a lighter value of the same hue (see Figure II.D.3).

Figure II.D.3
The textures and shadows in the lemons have been changed from black and white to various shades of a yellow hue.

Add more color depth and variety

Switch to the Airbrush tool by pressing **A**. Use a brush with Mode set to Multiply on the Airbrush Options palette and Pressure at 20%. Choose **Window➡Show Brushes** to open the Brushes palette and select a brush tip with a 100-pixel diameter, 0% Hardness, and 25% Spacing, and begin to paint several strokes on each lemon.

Change the foreground color to a bright lemon yellow. The example begins with Trumatch 12-a and then 11-b1 and 10-a are added in the strokes to achieve a variety of yellows and a hand-painted look (see Figure II.D.4).

Figure II.D.4
When used in the Multiply mode, airbrush strokes retain the shading and texture from the original painting.

Add shading to the lemons

Change the foreground color to a yellow green and choose a larger brush tip. The example here uses Trumatch 15-b as the foreground color, with a 200-pixel diameter brush and an Opacity setting of 10%.

Set Mode to Multiply and run the airbrush along the bottom and top edges of the lemons until they are darkened. If your light source is from the top, the lemons should be darkened more on the bottom. Switch back to the 100-pixel diameter brush to add some shading inside the lemons, around the protrusions for the stems, as shown in Figure II.D.5.

Figure II.D.5
Create a sense of volume by shading the outside edges of the lemons.

Figure II.D.6
Add white highlights to the lemons with an airbrush set to Normal mode and 10% Pressure.

Add white airbrush highlights

Now add highlights to the areas where the light reflects off the lemons. Choose the 200-pixel brush tip and set Pressure to 10%. Change the foreground color to white and Mode to Normal.

Carefully add highlights with the Airbrush to further increase the illusion of volume in the shape of the lemons, as shown in Figure II.D.6.

Darken and lighten areas with Dodge/Burn

Press **O** to switch to the Toning tools. With a 100-pixel diameter brush and an Exposure setting of 20% or less, lighten selected areas with the Dodge tool or darken areas with the Burn tool. Using these tools is different from spraying another coat of paint; rather than obscure the underlying textures, Toning tools heighten texture and contrast (see Figure II.D.7).

Figure II.D.7
Use the Dodge and Burn tools to darken and lighten selected areas without painting over them.

If you want to darken the shadow of the front two lemons onto the lemon behind them, load selections for the first two and then choose **Select➨Inverse**. This enables you to darken areas of the lemon in back without affecting the two in front.

Change the color of the stems

Switch to the Lasso tool by pressing **L**. Zoom in to a high level of magnification and draw around the edge of the stem with a Lasso. Change to the Toning tools by pressing **O**. Continue pressing **O** until you see the Sponge icon. On the Toning Tools Options palette, choose Desaturate and set Exposure to 20%. With a large brush, run the Sponge over the selected stem until it loses about half its coloration (desaturates). Then open **Image➨Adjust➨ Hue/Saturation** and move the Hue slider to the right until the stem takes on a slightly more green cast, as shown in Figure II.D.8.

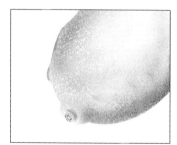

Figure II.D.8
Desaturate the stems on the lemons to remove some of the color; then add more green to the hue.

Figure II.b.11
Heighten the emotional color of the painting by adding different hues to the shadow areas.

Colorize the background shadows

The shadows cast by the lemons present an opportunity to add some emotional color. The example in this lesson uses colors that were not in the original model for the still life: a green cast for shadows in front of the lemons and violet for the deeper shadows behind them.

To colorize the shadows you made in the black-and-white painting, follow these steps:

1. Choose **Select➥Load Selection** and activate the selection for all three lemons.

2. Choose **Select➥Inverse** to select the background area rather than the lemons.

3. Change the foreground color to a dark green.

4. Choose a 400-pixel diameter Airbrush. On the Airbrush Options palette, set Pressure to 30% and highlight Overlay in the Blending Mode pull-down menu. Overlay mode adds color only to the darkest parts of the shadows, leaving the lighter areas untouched.

5. Drag the Airbrush over the front shadows that you want to take on a green color.

6. Switch to a violet and repeat the same process with the shadows behind the lemons.

After colorizing the original painting's shadows, you may want to add or remove some. If you add shadows, be sure to change the blending mode back to Normal and lower the Pressure setting to 10% or less. To remove portions of shadows, change the background color to white and toggle between it and the foreground color by pressing **X**. The example in Figure II.D.9 shows the shadows colorized by using the Overlay blending mode and then touched up with the Normal blending mode at low pressure with green, violet, and brown.

Suggest depth of field with blurred edges

When you look at a scene, you see sharper edges on the objects closest to you and more blurred edges on those in the distance. You can use this effect to create multiple levels of focus, which, in turn, help define the pictorial space and add visual interest to a painting.

Figure II.D.10
Blur the edges of objects in the background and sharpen the edges of those in the forefront.

Press **R** to switch to the Focusing tools. Continue pressing **R** until you see the Blur icon, which looks like a droplet. Set Pressure to 50%. Display the Brushes palette (**F5**) and choose the 13-pixel, soft–edged brush. Deselect the background so that your strokes will affect the entire painting. Zoom in to a high level of magnification and run the Blur tool over the top edge of the lemon in back several times to soften the contrast between it and the background. Then move to the two lemons in the forefront. Blur the edges where they meet the lemon behind them but not as much as before. Move down the sides of these lemons and blur them against their background a little, as shown in Figure II.D.10.

You may want to switch to the Sharpen tool by pressing **R** and trace around the edges in the forefront to increase the contrast somewhat. Be careful doing this because you can Sharpen too much and create a pixelated look that you don't want.

This concludes the lesson on adding color to your illustration of the lemons. You've learned how to colorize a black-and-white image with a single hue by using Hue/Saturation and individual elements such as the shadows by using brushes with different mode settings. In the process, you've seen the dramatic effect that adding a range of colors to a black-and-white composition can have.

Part III: Lesson A   Painting the pond with a "wash"

In this lesson, you fill the negative shape surrounding the boat with the pond water. The water presents an opportunity to bring atmosphere and mood to your painting; the way you paint its surface enables you to impact your viewer. Will you make the water clear or murky? Will it be full of shadows and mystery, or bright and reflective? Will it be still or rippled?

Painting the water requires the use of different techniques and brushes than those you used for painting the boat. Because it covers a larger

Art concepts

Negative shape

Color balance

Wash

Photoshop tools and features

Magic Wand tool

Tolerance levels

Layer masks

Custom brushes

Pen

Paintbrush

Smudge

Wave filter

Eyedropper

area and contains less detail, you can use very large brushes. Blending colors is also an important component.

If you were painting the pond with traditional watercolors, you would probably use what is known as a wash technique. This means blocking out the boat with a resistant film so you could paint with broad strokes and not worry about getting unwanted paint on the boat. The paint would be diluted, creating a semitransparent film of color.

You can imitate the wash technique in Photoshop by creating a mask layer for the boat and using very large brushes, hundreds of pixels in diameter. Set a low Opacity level for your Paintbrush and gain the control you would have with a true watercolor wash as you gradually build up areas of the pond.

Flatten the Image

Make sure that the Paper layer is visible and the sketch doesn't show through. Choose **Layer➡Flatten Image** to place the painted boat on the Background layer.

Select the gray area around the boat

Press **W** to change to the Magic Wand tool. Set the Wand's tolerance to 32 to ensure that you pick up the pixels around the boat's edge that were smudged and blended with other colors. A higher tolerance level ensures that more colors are selected. Click the Wand anywhere in the gray area surrounding the boat. Be sure that the entire area is selected and that none of the boat is selected. If the selection includes parts of the boat you don't want to paint, set a lower number for the tolerance level and try again.

Another technique to use if you want the selection to be closer to the boat's edge is to choose **Select➡Modify➡Expand** and enter a pixel value between 1 and 16, which expands the selection by the number of pixels you enter. Then click **OK**, switch the foreground color to white, and fill the selection.

Create a layer mask

Choose **Layer➡New➡Layer** and name it *Water*. Then select **Layer➡Add Layer Mask➡Reveal Selection**. This blocks the unselected area and prevents any of the broad wash strokes from flooding into the boat.

Figure III.A.1
Paint broad strokes of dark green using a large brush with the boat masked out.

Begin painting with a large custom brush

Click the Layer thumbnail to the left of the layer mask on the Layers palette. Change to the Paintbrush tool by pressing **B**. Add a new brush by clicking the first empty space of the Brushes palette and set Diameter at 200 pixels with 0% Hardness and 25% Spacing. Leave Angle and Roundness at their defaults. Select a dark green color and with Opacity set at 40%, and begin painting large curved strokes around the boat. You will quickly notice that the boat is not affected (see Figure III.A.1).

Now change to a different dark green and build up the strokes much as you did when painting the boat. Continue to alter the brush color, adding dark browns, olives, and dark gray to the top part of the picture, lighter grays, greens and browns near the bottom (see Figure III.A.2).

Figure III.A.2
Add brush strokes of different colors to build complexity.

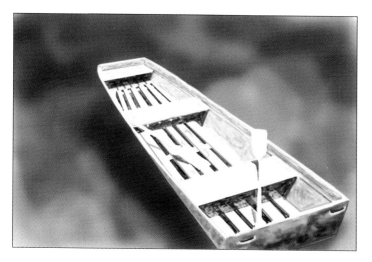

Figure III.A.3
Paint in blues to represent the reflection of the sky in the water.

Add more detail with a smaller custom brush

Add another new brush, this time 125–150 pixels in diameter, with all other settings the same. Change the Opacity setting to 60% to allow the blues to contrast more against the dark green colors. Choose a light blue and begin painting the large area of blue on the boat's right side, as shown in Figure III.A.3. Switch to a darker blue and paint the large area of blue to the left.

Define the shadow on the left of the boat

The shadow along the left side of the boat is more dominant than the other shadows, so it should have a harder edge. Press **P** to change to the Pen tool and click at the point where the shadow meets the top of the boat. Click again, drag out a short handle, and again where shadow meets the bottom of the picture plane. Click again where the shadow meets the boat at the bottom of the picture, and then click back where you started to complete the path. Don't worry about carefully defining the shadow edge where it meets the boat; that is already being done by the Layer mask. Click the third circle from the left on the bottom of the Paths palette to make the path you've drawn an active selection, and you have defined an area for painting the shadow.

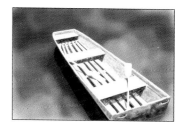

Figure III.A.4
Define a path and make the selection active to paint the boat's shadow.

Change to the Paintbrush by pressing **B** and change your brush to the 100 pixel, soft-edged tip in the Brushes palette, with Opacity at 40%. Paint in the shadow area with a variety of dark blues and dark grays (not black) (see Figure III.A.4).

Figure III.A.5
Smudge colors from one area to another to suggest ripples.

Figure III.A.6
Use the Eyedropper to pick up colors from an area and the Paintbrush to create more ripples.

Smudge colors to suggest ripples

Study the ripple patterns in the original photograph carefully. Consider how they might have been caused: Are they the result of a soft breeze, or are they left from the boy rocking the boat? The ripples present an opportunity to add to the story being told in your painting.

Change to the Smudge tool by pressing **U**. Choose a 45-pixel or smaller soft-edged brush and 60% Opacity. In areas where blue and green meet, smudge first from the green into the blue; then into the blue from the green. Follow the general directions of the ripples in the photograph, or make your own patterns. Carefully control the smudge you make into the edge of the darkest shadow (see Figure III.A.5).

Paint in more ripples

Press **I** and pick up a color from the light blue area with the Eyedropper tool. Switch to the Paintbrush tool and select a smaller soft-edged brush, 25 to 30 pixels in diameter, and set Opacity to 90%. Use this brush to paint and define the smaller ripples. Switch back to the Eyedropper tool to pick up another color, such as dark green, which can be painted into the blue areas. These strokes might look a little too bold at this point, but you can correct that in the next step (see Figure III.A.6).

Soften the ripple strokes with the Wave filter

Switch to the Lasso tool by pressing **L**. Draw an irregular line around the ripples you just painted on the left of the boat to select them. Choose **Filter➥Distort➥Wave**, and you see a wide array of dialog box settings. Experiment with different combinations of the Number of Generators, Minimum/Maximum Wavelength, Amplitude, Horizontal/Vertical Scale, Repeat Edge Pixels, and Wrap Around Undefined Areas settings. There are also choices for wave type—Sine, Triangle, or Square—and a Randomize option.

Use the trial and error method to achieve your desired effect. The Wave filter and all the other global filters can make alterations that range from subtle to profound; experiment with different levels to find the right look for your style.

Select an area of the ripples on the right and apply the Wave effect again with similar settings, but alter the direction of the wave so that it's perpendicular to the direction of most of the strokes (see Figure III.A.7).

Balance the boat and pond colors

At this point, a disparity exists between the colors used in the boat and those in the pond. The rich, luminous blues and greens of the water seem to have no relation to the stark grays, bright whites, and other colors in the boat. To unify the painting, you can add a light blue wash to the boat:

1. Make the Background layer the active layer.

2. Change to the Eyedropper tool by pressing **I**. Click the Eyedropper on an area containing a light, bright blue in the water to make that the foreground color.

3. Choose **Edit➥Fill**, and when the dialog box appears, use the Foreground color with the Opacity set at 3%.

Evaluate how this changes the composition by pressing **Command-Z** (Macintosh) or **Ctrl-Z** (Windows) to Undo the fill, and then again to Redo it. You may want to increase or decrease the Opacity level or change the color you're using for the fill.

You can also use some of the dark green from the water and paint some shadows along the sides of the oars with a small, soft-edged brush with a 30% or lower Opacity.

Finally, you can use some of the darker blues from the water to change the color of the black shadows beneath the seats and between the slats. Choose a dark blue and paint over the shadow areas using a small soft-edged brush and Opacity lower than 20%.

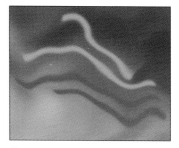

Figure III.A.7
Add realism to the water's surface by using the Wave filter.

Figure III.A.8
The Smudge tool can be used to touch up rough areas of the painting.

Touch up rough areas using the Smudge tool

Zoom in to a high level of magnification and inspect your painting closely. There may be areas where too much white shows through, a line is too harsh, or colors are not well blended. The Smudge tool is ideal for working on these areas. Press **U** to switch to the Smudge tool and carefully apply it to the areas you want to work on. Use 50% or lower Opacity and appropriately sized brush tips.

If, for example, you're blending a line such as that shown in Figure III.A.8, use a small brush; if you're softening strokes in a large area, use a larger tip. You might need to smudge the outline of the entire boat against the water; you can use short smudge strokes constrained by holding down the **Shift** key to keep the smudges from becoming wavy.

Now that you've painted the water, you have taken the image from a simple study of a boat to something much more evocative with just a few simple effects. In later lessons, you learn how to alter colors to change the atmosphere of your painting.

You might like to save this file for output. If so, choose **Save As** and give it a new name. Flatten the layers and change the mode to CMYK. Save it as a TIFF file, which you can send to an IRIS printer or other output device.

Part III: Lesson B   Using an "oil painting" technique

Oil paint is one of the oldest and most traditional of all art mediums. Its popularity stems from its deep, rich colors, its permanence, and the way it enables the artist to build up layer after layer, working and reworking the painting to build interest with texture.

Oils lend themselves well to every painting style from realism to abstract expressionism. The

Art concepts

Realism

Abstract Expressionism

Additive process

Painting surface

Photoshop tools and features

Layers

Fresco filter

Eraser tool

texture on the painting surface can range from smooth to very rough and tactile. Brush strokes can be tight and controlled, or very loose and impetuous.

In this lesson, you'll use your self-portrait and apply some Photoshop techniques that will suggest the rich, complex beauty of a traditional oil painting.

Open portrait painting and save a copy

Open the version of your working file for the pastel self portrait that you saved before you applied the Rough Pastels filter in Part II, Lesson C. Choose **Save As**, and give the file a new name. Be sure you are working in RGB Color.

Add a background to your portrait

If you haven't done so already, add a background to your portrait. It is unusual (though of course, not unheard of) for oil paintings to have large areas of unpainted canvas showing.

The example in Figure III.B.1 uses neutral background colors containing a lot of grays, in order to provide contrast with the more colorful portrait image.

Figure III.B.1
Add a background to fill the empty areas of your painting surface.

Figure III.B.2
The results of the Fresco Artistic filter and Fade filter in Overlay mode.

Apply the Fresco filter

Simply applying a filter, even to a complex painting that you have carefully built up brush stroke by brush stroke, will yield a programmed, "automatic" look. You can mitigate this by applying filters and then erasing some of their effects with a semitransparent eraser. Therefore, before applying the Fresco Artistic filter, choose **Layer➡Duplicate Layer** so you can erase back into your unfiltered layer.

Select **Filter➡Artistic➡Fresco**, and when the dialog box appears, enter these values for settings: Brush Size 2, Brush Detail 8, Texture 2. Click OK, and then choose **Filter➡Fade Fresco**. When the dialog box appears, leave Opacity at 100% and change Mode to Overlay. The brush strokes in your portrait will change to resemble the example in Figure III.B.2.

Erase through to background layer

Change to the Eraser tool by pressing **E**. Set Opacity at 50%, make Wet Edges active, and choose the 35-pixel diameter brush tip. Begin to erase away some of the Fresco filter layer. Change Opacity settings for the Eraser, as well as brush tip sizes as you work to give a more varied appearance to your eraser strokes. Overlap strokes, and vary their length and direction.

Erasing in this way, by building up the effects of the Eraser through varying Opacity and Wet Edges helps give your painting a more natural, hand-crafted appearance. As you develop more stroke complexity, the painting becomes more interesting than it would be with just the simple application of a filter. (Figure III.B.3)

Figure III.B.3
Use the Eraser tool with varying Opacity levels and Wet Edges to build more interesting strokes.

Add and erase through a layer of white

Now add even more complexity and texture to your painting by adding and then selectively removing a layer of white. Make another layer and fill it with 100% white. Use the Eraser tool as you did before to remove the white. Start with the Eraser set to 40% Opacity, and select Wet Edges. Use a 35-pixel diameter soft-edged brush tip, and build up the effect by overlapping strokes of varying lengths, in different directions, beginning with the nose and eyes of your face (see Figure III.B.4).

Figure III.B.4
Cover the painting with a layer of white and erase back to begin revealing brush strokes underneath.

Merge layers and apply a canvas texture filter

Oil paintings are typically painted on stretched canvas, the preparation of which is the first step the artist takes. With Photoshop, creating the canvas texture is the final step.

Save a your finished oil portrait, then make a copy of the file you've been working on to use for this step. Flatten all the layers in the file copy, and choose **Filter➦Texture➦Texturizer**, and when the dialog box appears, enter the following settings: Texture: Canvas, Scaling 100%, Relief 2, Light Dir: Top. Click **OK**, and your portrait will now look like it was painted on stretched canvas. (Figure III.B.5)

Figure III.B.05
Make the portrait look more like an oil painting by applying a canvas texture with a filter.

Oil paintings depend on what's called the additive process—a careful building up of strokes—to achieve their interesting texture and complexity. In this lesson you've learned Photoshop techniques that are the equivalent of this process. There is no substitute for individually laid down strokes, whether they are made with solid colors and a paintbrush or a filtered layer erased away in stages.

If you want to output your self-portrait at this stage, save a copy as a CMYK TIFF.

Part III: Lesson C   **Expanding the lemons painting**

In this lesson, you'll impart more of a story to your lemon still life by adding some new elements. A successful still life is more than a group of objects sitting together; it should be a slice of life. Adding a mug and a wedge of lemon to your composition

Art concepts

Volume

Light

Reflectivity

Balance

Contrast

Photoshop tools and features

Layers

ties the otherwise unrelated elements together by implying that someone is preparing to add some lemon juice into a mug of tea.

The mug also provides a chance to add some reflections to the scene to make it richer. Reflections are created when illumination shines onto a form from another surface. Unless the reflection is in a flat mirror, it will be distorted by the shape of the form. As you paint reflections, always pay close attention to these distortions as you see them in the subject matter, rather than the shape of the object being reflected. This means the painted reflection will be more abstract, and its colors and texture will be strongly influenced by the strength of light and the form reflecting it.

As you add elements to your still life subject matter, think about balance. Arrange the new objects in such a way that you create some tension in the equilibrium of the composition. Placing the mug in the middle of the picture, for example, would make the composition *too* balanced, whereas setting it off to the side as shown here gives the scene more of a sense of movement.

Arrange your scene

Begin by placing a white piece of paper and the three lemons next to your computer in the same positions as in the original painting. If a lot of time has elapsed since you did the painting, use new lemons that are roughly the same size and shape as the originals. Don't worry about small differences; remember, you'll be painting the *reflection* of the lemons, not the lemons themselves.

Next, set a coffee mug behind the three lemons. If possible, it should be of a basic straight-sided, coffee-shop model, in a solid color. Not only will this kind of mug be easier to draw, but painting the reflections on its surface will be easier as well. Because you'll be concentrating on painting the reflective surface of the mug, you may want to add more sheets of white paper around the composition to block out other reflections from your desktop. To tie the mug and the lemons together as a "story," slice a wedge from another lemon and place it near the mug. Also, light the composition in the same way you did before.

Enlarge the canvas size

To comfortably fit the mug and lemon wedge in your composition, you need to expand the canvas. Open the lemons still life and change the Background color on the Photoshop toolbox to white. Choose **Image➡Canvas Size**, and when the dialog box appears, change Height from four to six inches. Then click the middle box on the bottom row of the group of nine squares and arrows as seen here to place the lemons at the bottom, rather than the middle of the new canvas (see Figure III.C.1).

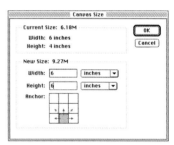

Figure III.C.1
You can increase the size of your canvas to add more room for painting.

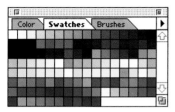

Figure III.C.2
Add more colors to your Swatches palette to paint the mug.

Add the mug's colors to your palette

Begin by loading the Swatches palette you originally used to paint the lemons. To paint the mug, you'll need all its colors you see in your palette. Examine your mug closely. It contains many more colors besides just the one it "appears" to be at first glance. Choose one specific hue for the mug's basic color, and also take note of the range of light to dark colors you see in the shadows and highlights. Then look for the colors of the lemons reflected in its surface.

Adding colors to a palette is covered in Part II, Lesson A. Follow the steps outlined there for building a palette using the Trumatch color system and add colors until you have the full range of tones and hues needed to paint the mug and the reflections of the lemons in it.

The mug used in the example is dark blue, and the colors added to the Swatches palette are all tonal variations of that blue, from lightest to darkest (see Figure III.C.2).

Create a new layer and a layer mask

Choose **Layer➡New➡Layer** and name it *Mug*. Make the selection for the lemons active and then choose **Layer➡Add Layer Mask➡Hide Selection**. This blocks the lemons from the areas you'll be airbrushing and enables you to paint over the shading behind them when you add the mug to the composition.

Outline and color the inside of the mug

Click the Mug layer thumbnail located to the left of the Layer mask thumbnail on the Layers palette. Now change to the Marquee tool by pressing **M**. Continue to press **M** until the elliptical Marquee is selected. Then click and drag an oval to represent the rim of the mug. More than likely, in your view of the mug, the oval defining the rim will be at an angle, but for now, do not rotate it.

Throughout this lesson, you'll be asked to use the mug's basic color. To decide what color this is, think of the mug without shadows or highlights, and change the foreground color to that which most closely represents the overall color of your mug. Select **Edit➞Fill**, and, with Opacity set to 100%, fill the oval with the foreground color by pressing the **Return** key (Macintosh) or **Enter** key (Windows).

Rotate and save the filled oval

After the oval is filled, choose **Layer➞Transform➞Rotate**. Click one of the handles which appear, and drag the oval so that it's at a slight angle. Press the **Return** (Macintosh) or **Enter** key (Windows) to apply the rotation. This will give your composition a more realistic appearance than a perfectly level view (see Figure III.C.3).

After you have rotated the selected oval, be sure to save its shape by choosing **Select➞Save Selection**. This way, you'll be able to isolate it from the rest of the mug later on when you'll be adding more airbrush strokes for shading and highlights.

Define the bottom edge of the mug

It will be easier to paint the mug if you turn off the view of the lemons. To do this, open the Layers palette by choosing **Window➞Show Layers** and click the Eye icon next to the small view of the lemons. This hides the background and lets you get a better sense of the proportions and shape of the mug. Be sure your layer has white as the transparency color.

Load the selection of the oval, copy it, and paste it. Switch to the Move tool by pressing **V**. Click the oval, press the **Shift** key to keep it aligned with the first oval, and drag it down until the bottom of the new oval is in the correct position to define the bottom of the mug (see Figure III.C.4).

Figure III.C.3
Use the Marquee tool to define the top rim of the mug, fill it with color and rotate it slightly.

Figure III.C.4
Use a copy of the oval you made for the top to define the bottom of the mug.

Figure III.C.5
The basic shape of the mug has been outlined and filled.

Define and color the sides of the mug

To fill in the area between the two ovals, follow these steps:

1. Switch to the Pen tool by pressing **P**. Click the left-outside edge of the top oval to begin a line for the edge.

2. Hold the **Shift** key to keep the line vertical, and click the outside edge of the bottom oval.

3. Release the **Shift** key, and click the right edge of the bottom oval. Then hold **Shift** again, and click the right edge of the top oval. Finally, release the **Shift** key, and click the starting point to complete a parallelogram.

4. Open the Paths palette, and click the Make Selection icon (third from the left) to make the parallelogram an active selection. Then click the Trash icon to delete the path.

5. Switch to the Magic Wand tool by pressing **W**. Hold the **Shift** key again to retain the active selection and click the Wand anywhere on the bottom oval. This adds it to the selection.

6. Save this selection, and choose **Edit➡Fill** to fill it with the same color as the first oval when you press the **Return** (Macintosh) or **Enter** key (Windows). Then choose **Select➡None**.

7. Press **Command-E** (Macintosh) or **Ctrl-E** (Windows) to merge all the elements into the Mug layer. Reveal the background layer to see the relationship of the mug to the lemons (see Figure III.C.5).

Outline and color the mug's handle

Change to the Pen tool by pressing **P**. Draw the basic outline of the mug's handle with the Pen (see Figure III.C.6). When you have the shape you want, display the Paths palette and make the outline an active selection by clicking the third circle from the left at the bottom of the palette. Now save the handle selection, delete the path you drew, choose **Edit➡Fill**, and press the **Return** (Macintosh) or **Enter** key (Windows). The handle will be filled with the foreground color. Then deselect the handle by choosing **Select➡None**. If you haven't done so already, this is a good time to save your file.

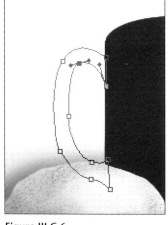

Figure III.C.6
Define a path and make the selection active to create the mug's handle.

Now that you've created the basic shape for the mug, it's time to make it look three-dimensional by painting in shadows, highlights, and reflections. The Airbrush is an ideal tool for this purpose.

Paint shadows and highlights in the handle

Now choose the Airbrush tool by pressing **A**. Open the Airbrush Options palette, and set Pressure to 40%, mode to Normal. Select a very dark hue of the mug's basic color in the Swatches palette as the foreground color, and then change to the Brushes palette and choose the 65-pixel diameter, soft-edged brush tip. With the handle selection active, use the dark color to add the shadows. If the shadows appear too heavy, switch back to the basic mug color, fill the selection with it, and try again using either a lighter hue or lower Pressure setting.

117

Figure III.C.7
Paint the shadows and highlights on the mug's handle using the Airbrush and Pen tools.

After you've painted in the shadows, you can add the bright highlights. If you look at your subject matter, you'll probably see highlights following the curve of the handle, and notice that their thickness does not vary markedly. If you tried to paint these thin, curved lines freehand, you'd probably find it difficult to do without having wavy lines, which wouldn't look like highlights on a smooth surface. To easily paint the curved lines to define highlights, follow these steps:

1. Select the Pen tool by pressing **P**. Click where you want the highlight to begin, and without moving the mouse, click again to draw out a tangent handle.

2. Click at the point where you wish the highlight line to end. You can press the **Control** key (Macintosh) or **Ctrl** key (Windows) to change to the pointer tool and adjust the line's length, position or curve by clicking either the line itself, its endpoints, or its tangents.

3. Open the Brushes palette and choose a smaller, soft-edged brush, 35 pixels in diameter or less.

4. Press **A** to change to the Airbrush, and set Pressure at 20%.

5. Switch from the Brushes palette to the Swatches palette, and change the foreground color to white or a very light hue of the mug's basic color.

6. Display the Paths palette, and stroke (add paint color to) the line you have drawn by clicking the second circle from the left on the bottom of the palette. You may have to stroke the line more than once to obtain the highlight color you want.

If you are not happy with the look of your shadows or highlights, you can change the foreground color back to the basic mug color and, with a large brush tip and low Pressure setting use the Airbrush to tone down the darker and lighter hues. Of course, you can always choose **Edit➥Fill** to return the handle to the base color, and begin painting the shadows and highlights again.

Paint reflections in the outside of the mug

Now load the selection for the outside of the mug. As you paint the reflections in the mug, disregard the fact that they are filling in the top oval for now because later you'll select the top oval and paint its shadows separately. Press **Return** (Macintosh) or **Enter** (Windows) to display the Airbrush Options palette. Lower the Pressure setting to 30%.

Open the Brushes palette and create a new brush with a 300 pixel diameter, 0% Hardness, and 25% Spacing. Change to the Swatches palette, and choose a lighter hue of your basic mug color. To paint the vertical reflection of the light on the side of the mug, click once above the point where you want the airbrush stroke to begin, hold the **Shift** key, and click below the bottom of the mug. This produces a vertical highlight.

Now change your brush to a 200-pixel diameter, and apply another stroke over the first one, again using the **Shift** key. This makes the highlight brighter in the middle. Finally, change to the 65-pixel brush, and make a third stroke. This process will yield a realistic looking reflection as seen in Figure III.C.8.

Figure III.C.8
A vertical highlight suggests light striking the curve of the outside of the mug.

Add the handle reflection

Switch to a foreground color that's a darker hue of your basic mug color. Lower the Airbrush Pressure setting to 10% and start with a 35-pixel diameter brush to paint the darker reflection of the handle, which you can do freehand. Then choose the next largest brush, 65 pixels, and paint over the first stroke. Proceed to the 100-pixel brush and stroke a third time.

When you're satisfied with the dark strokes for the handle's reflection, switch the foreground color to a hue that is lighter than the basic color and set the Airbrush Pressure to 5%. Choose a very small brush, such as 13 pixels, and carefully add some bright highlights in the reflection of the handle.

Figure III.C.9
Painting the rim a lighter color and adding highlights to the inside of the mug enhances the illusion of three dimensions.

Add the shadows inside the mug

Load the selection for the top oval (the inside of the mug). Fill the oval with the basic mug color at 100% Opacity to erase any portion of the painted side from the previous steps that may have filled part of the oval. Switch to the 100-pixel diameter brush, and set the Airbrush Pressure at 20%. Begin with a color that is slightly darker than the basic mug color, and brush in broad strokes for shadows. Choose a darker hue, and build up the shadows gradually, continuing to use darker colors until you get to black for a final series of strokes near the bottom edge.

Paint the rim of the mug and add highlights

To make the mug seem more three-dimensional, paint a lighter color rim around the top edge by choosing **Select➡Modify➡ Border** and entering a value of 20 pixels when the dialog box appears. Switch the foreground color to a very light hue of the basic mug color, and use a small brush tip and low pressure setting for the Airbrush. Zoom in to a high level of magnification, and carefully paint a brighter color in just the bottom part of the selected oval.

Load the selection for the original oval again, and finally, with a small airbrush and a low Pressure setting, add highlights near the top edge of the inside of the mug, as seen in Figure III.C.9.

Add the lemon reflections to the mug

Study your subject for the reflection of the lemons in the mug. Press **L** to change to the Lasso tool. Draw a rough outline similar to the distorted shape of the first lemon as it appears in the reflection. Choose the Rubber Stamp tool by pressing **S**, and press **Return** (Macintosh) or **Enter** (Windows) to open the Rubber Stamp Options palette. Set Opacity at 10%, Mode at Clone (Non-aligned) and check the Sample Merged box.

Open the Brushes palette, and choose a 200- or 300-pixel diameter brush. Hold the **Option** (Macintosh) or **Alt** key (Windows), and click a bright, heavily textured part of the lemons. Then release the **Option/Alt** key, and stamp inside the selected area of the mug where you want to suggest the lemon's reflection. Repeat this process two or three times until you build up enough of the appearance of the lemon to look like it's reflected in the mug (see Figure III.C.10).

Figure III.C.10
The Rubber Stamp tool set at very low Opacity can be used to suggest the reflected lemons.

Paint the lemon wedge

It's time to add the wedge of cut lemon that will help tie the composition together by telling a "story." As you paint the lemon wedge, you'll make use of the same tools and features you've been using all along: the Pen tool, saved selections, and the Airbrush.

At this point, you can merge the mug layer with the background layer by pressing **Command-E** (Macintosh) or **Ctrl-E** (Windows). Now, add a new layer named Lemon Wedge.

First, switch to the Lasso tool by pressing **L**. Draw the basic half-moon shape of the lemon wedge's rind. Save the selection, change the foreground color to white or very light gray, and fill the selection. Next, make the foreground color a slightly darker gray, and switch to the Airbrush tool by pressing **A**. Set Pressure at 20%, and Mode to Dissolve on the Airbrush Options palette. Select the 65-pixel diameter soft-edged brush, and paint a few strokes of texture towards the outside edge of the rind.

Figure III.C.11
Add a lemon wedge to tie the lemons and mug together as *rrrrgi*

Change back to the Lasso tool and sketch in the juicy inside of the lemon wedge. Save this selection, and change the foreground color to a very pale yellow. With a 200-pixel diameter Airbrush at 60% Pressure, paint in the yellow area. Then switch to white, lower the Pressure of the Airbrush to 20%, and add highlights in the middle of the lemon wedge.

Switch to a very small airbrush with just 10% Pressure, choose a light brown, and add numerous strokes to suggest the fibers. Then change back to white, raise Pressure to 60%, and paint in more fibers.

Use the Lasso tool to draw the outside of the rind, which shows on the underside of the lemon wedge, and save the selection. Change to the Rubber Stamp tool by pressing **S**. Set Opacity at 100%, Mode to Clone (Non-aligned), check Sample Merged, hold the **Option** key (Macintosh) or the **Alt** key (Windows) and click a dark area of one of the whole lemons. Release the Opt/Alt key, and use the Stamp tool to paint the rind in the selected area. Finally, add details, such as a seed, using a small Airbrush until the lemon wedge looks similar to the one seen in Figure III.C.11.

Now return your attention to the background, and paint in the shadows cast by the new elements you've added. This will tie your painting together. Finally, use the Toning tools and Smudge tool to smooth out the rough edges and add a sense of dimension by blurring edges in the distance.

Paint in the mug and wedge shadows

Merge the layers again so that everything is on the background layer. Load the selections of the entire mug, adding all three lemons and the lemon wedge to the selection. Save this grouped selection as a new selection, and then choose **Select→Inverse** to make the background the active selection.

Use large, soft-edged Airbrushes from 200 to 500 pixels in diameter, with Pressure of 20%, and the same dark colors you used to paint the shadows under the original lemons. Add a dark shadow under the lemon wedge and lighter shadows around the top of the mug.

Use Smudge and Blur tools for final touch-up

Deselect the inverted background selection, and make sure no other elements are selected. Press **S** to change to the Smudge tool. Set opacity at 50%, choose a very small, soft-edged brush tip, about 13 pixels, and zoom in to a high level of magnification. Carefully examine areas where elements meet the background, and make sure no unpainted pixels are showing through. If some are, smudge the correct color into those areas.

Finally, change to the Blur tool by pressing **R**. Switch to a 45-pixel diameter, soft-edged brush tip, and set Opacity at 100%. Make numerous passes over the top of the mug, around the handle, and around the lemon wedge to blur them into the background. Remember that the edges of objects in the foreground should be blurred less, and those in the distance should be blurred more.

With the skills you have developed in this lesson, you'll be able to rework the composition of your digital paintings by adding, moving, and refining the elements that comprise your subject matter. If you're careful to always save paths and selections, and work in layers with masks, you'll be able to move objects around in a painting as easily as you can move them on your desktop.

Part III: Lesson D   Making architectural textures

In Part I, you learned to use Photoshop's tools to make a simple drawing of a door. Architectural illustrations often rely on textures to make them appear more realistic. Wood, brick, stone, marble, metal, glass, and concrete are just a few of the many textures you can use in drawing and painting architecture.

Often, textures such as these are available as backgrounds from stock photo or clip art sup-

Art concepts

Texture

Color combinations

Tonality

Shading

Reflectivity

Photoshop tools and features

Clouds filter

Wave filter

Layers

Gradients

pliers, but because the focus of this book is creating original art, in this lesson you'll learn how to make and apply some of these textures. Besides that, you'll want to avoid the adding the "prefab" look of somebody else's textures when you're making original fine art.

To make your painting convincing, you must choose the right textures for your door. Perhaps, as in the example, your door is wood, or maybe it's glass or metal. As you learn about creating these textures, experiment with how you can use Photoshop's many tools to blend and filter colors for the best effect.

Change to RGB mode

Open your original working file for the door drawing, choose **Save As**, and give the file a new name. At first your palette will be displayed in grayscale. Choose **Image➡Mode➡RGB Color**, and the palette will default back to color. Now you're ready to make the woodgrain texture and add it.

Add a new layer for the woodgrain

Make a new layer called *Woodgrain*, and follow these steps to produce the texture:

1. Change the foreground color to a light tan (the color in Figure III.D.1's example uses R129, G198, B173) and the background color to dark brown (R82, G49, B24).

2. Select **Filter➡Render>Clouds** to create a random blend of the foreground and background colors as seen in Figure III.D.1.

3. Choose **Filter>Distort➡Wave**, and enter the following settings: Generators, 35; Type, Sine; Min/Max Wave-lengths, 85/279; Min/Max Amplitudes, 15/384; Horiz/Vert Scale, 1%/100%; and Undefined Areas, Wrap Around.

4. Click **OK**, and the Wave filter will create the woodgrain for you (see Figure III.D.2).

If you find you don't have enough RAM to apply the Wave filter, (or any other filter) you can use a workaround. Select **Window➡Show Channels**, and when the Channels palette opens, select the first channel (Red). Apply the filter, and then switch to the next channel and press **Command-F** (Macintosh) or **Ctrl-F** (Windows) to apply the filter to it. Finally, choose the third channel (Blue), and apply the filter again. This has the same effect as applying the filter to all channels at once, and will take less RAM.

Figure III.D.1
Begin the woodgrain pattern by using the Clouds filter.

Figure III.D.2
Apply the Wave filter to create a woodgrain pattern.

Figure III.D.3
Delete the woodgrain from outside the door, and from other areas where it is unwanted.

Add complexity to the woodgrain

Using such algorithms as the Clouds and Wave filters on large areas of a painting can yield a programmed, repetitive appearance. You can add complexity to make your woodgrain more convincing by adding another layer with slightly different settings and orientation, and then blending it with the first layer. Start by repeating the steps above with slight alterations in the settings for the Wave filter and a different (but similar) pair of foreground/background colors.

After creating the second layer of woodgrain, choose **Layer➡ Transform➡Rotate 180°**. You may also wish to move the layer to the left or right a few pixels.

Make the second layer semi-transparent by adjusting the Opacity slider on the Layers palette between the range of 20% and 40%, so you see a blend of the two woodgrains. When you are satisfied with the appearance of the woodgrain, merge both layers by pressing **Command-E** (Macintosh) or **Ctrl-E** (Windows).

Delete gray fill and extra woodgrain texture

Load and select the path for the outer edge of the door, and make the layer active that contains the gray fill for the door. Delete the gray fill. Then change to the *Woodgrain* layer, choose **Select➡Inverse** and delete the woodgrain around the door. Next, load selections for areas such as the door handle or window panes, and delete the wood pattern from those as well (see Figure III.D.3).

Alter the woodgrain pattern in specific areas

Avoid having all woodgrain texture in the same direction and in the same colors unless your door is made from a solid piece of wood. The example door's decorative molding, for instance, is made from finish strips that are separate from the bulk of the door, so they should have woodgrain in a different color and direction. Also, shadows and highlights will alter the color of these surfaces on different planes.

Load selections for detail areas, and switch to the Smudge tool by pressing **U**. Using a small brush tip and Opacity set to about 80%, smooth away the underlying woodgrain. Then press **A** to change to the Airbrush tool, and with the smallest brush tip and 50% Opacity, choose a color that can suggest woodgrain in the right direction.

For larger areas that need woodgrain in a different direction, select and copy a portion of texture larger than you'll need, make a new layer, paste the selection and choose **Layer➡Transform➡Rotate** to change the direction of the grain. Click and drag the selection into position, and use the Eraser tool to trim the edges.

Continue to use the Smudge and Airbrush tools to handpaint the woodgrain in small areas. You may also wish to apply a filter, such as Ripple or Wave (see Figure III.D.4).

Figure III.D.4
Create a more realistic appearance by varying the direction of woodgrain in different portions of the door.

Create the glass texture

When you paint your door's glass, remember that it has a smooth, reflective texture. It can either be transparent, in which case objects on the other side of the glass will show through, or completely reflective. The example's glass is painted as if reflecting a blue sky.

To recreate this effect, begin with a new layer. Then load paths for the window panes, and make them active selections. Switch to the Gradient tool by pressing **G**. Open the Gradient Options palette, set Mode as Normal, Opacity at 50%, and Type as Linear.

Figure III.D.5
Glass is easy to suggest using Photoshop gradients.

Change the foreground color to light blue (R218, G211, B12) and the background color to white. Click and drag the Gradient tool at an angle across the pane of glass. Fill all panes separately, with the gradient in the same direction.

Now switch to the Airbrush tool by pressing **A**. Choose a 65-pixel diameter brush tip, and set Pressure at 30%. Press **X** to make white the foreground color. Make light airbrush streaks on the glass (see Figure III.D.5).

Creating metallic finishes

With the wood and glass panels finished, you're ready to turn to the door's hardware. The example's doorknob is painted in a brass color, with a brushed metal effect. To design a similar one for your door, follow these steps:

1. Make a new layer, and draw a rectangle over the door knob and plate. Fill this rectangle with medium gray (R150, G150, B150).

2. Select **Filter➡Noise➡Add Noise**. Change the settings to Amount 70, with Uniform Distribution, and check Monochromatic. Click OK.

3. Load the selection for the door handle, and make it active. Invert the selection, and delete area outside the door knob plate. Invert the selection again.

4. Change the foreground color to a gold (R218, G211, B12) Choose the Overlay blend mode on the Layers palette's pull-down menu. Select **Edit➡Fill**, and color the door handle and door handle plate (see Figure III.D.6).

Add shadows, highlights, and details

As with all Photoshop illustrations, take a moment to survey your composition for rough edges, areas that need darkening or lightening, and those that need more intricate detail. Zoom in to a high level of magnification, and use such tools as the Airbrush, Paintbrush, Smudge, Eraser, or Rubber Stamp to make the necessary changes.

Figure III.D.6
As seen in the doorknob, gradients are also useful for suggesting the reflectivity of metallic surfaces.

Creating fine art based on architecture offers an opportunity to study the effects of light and shadow, proportions and planes, and surface textures. In Part IV, you'll learn how to infuse even more interest to your painting of the door by adding context and drama.

Part IV: Lesson A Changing the boat painting

This lesson is about creative experimentation. Part of the appeal of using Photoshop to create fine art is that you can try out an effect and undo it if you don't like the results. Nothing becomes "permanent" until you save your file.

First you'll experiment with various ways to change the atmosphere of the boat and pond painting from Part III, Lesson A.

The landscape seen here was originally painted to represent a bright, summer afternoon. In this lesson, you'll learn to change your painting to

Art concepts

Atmosphere

Texture

Light and shadow

Photoshop tools and features

Loading selections

Adjusting curves

Lighting effects filter

Variations command

a night scene by casting the glow of an imaginary moon onto the boat and making the water dark and murky. In another variation, you'll see how to change the season from summer to fall by replacing some of the greens with reds and oranges to represent autumn leaves reflected on the pond's water. (If your landscape is already a fall or night scene, choose a different atmosphere for these exercises and adjust how you apply the principles described.)

When you've decided how you want your final composition to look, you can use a Photoshop filter to create the illusion that you painted it on real, rough watercolor paper.

Make a working file

To guard against one of your experiments failing and destroying your previous work, keep a copy of the boat painting in its original format and make new working files. Choose **Save As**, and give the new file a different name. Use RGB mode for the working file.

Work in only one layer for these exercises. This will help minimize file size, enable more memory-hungry filters to work, and simulate the experience of working on a real painting—where there are no "layers." If you saved your landscape with a channel for the boat selection, you can load the selection to isolate the effects explored here. If necessary, you can use the Pen tool and quickly trace the boat to save it as a selection.

Cast moonlight on the boat

Load the selection of the boat by choosing **Select➡Load Selection** and identifying the proper channel. When the boat is an active selection, choose **Filter➡Render➡Lighting Effects** to open the Lighting Effects palette (Figure IV.A.1). Be sure Preview is checked, so you can evaluate what happens as you adjust and combine various settings.

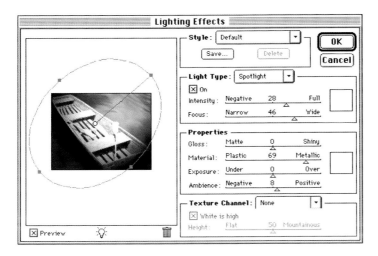

Figure IV.A.1
The Lighting Effects palette has a variety of settings that can be altered to create just the right effect. The circle with the radius can be moved or resized to alter where the light hits the boat.

Figure IV.A.2
After adjusting some settings and applying the Lighting Effects filter, the boat appears to be lit by moonlight.

You'll probably want the entire boat to be lit to some degree so that parts of it do not fade off into total darkness. You can move the definition points on the boat's preview image to redirect, reposition, expand, or contract the amount of light that falls on it. There are many styles and types of lights you can use, with settings that can be adjusted for such properties as color, gloss, material, exposure, and ambience.

The number of different Lighting Effects combinations can be bewildering; the only way to get the effect you want is to experiment, and when you think you have the settings correct, click OK. If you don't like what happens to your picture, you can Undo and try again.

For the lighting effects in Figure IV.A.2, we used the Default Style, with Spotlight as the Light Type. We increased Intensity and widened Focus to make the light more like that of the moon. We left the Gloss midway between Matte and Shiny, and shifted Material away from Plastic towards Metallic because, after all, the boat is aluminum. We didn't alter Exposure; Under exposure would make it too dark, and Over exposure would brighten it to the point where detail would be lost.

Darken the water

You can't have a moonlit boat and bright morning water; you need to mute it. Change the active selection from the boat to the water by choosing **Select➡Inverse**. Then select **Image➡Adjust➡ Curves** to open the Curves dialog box. (Figure IV.A.3). Click the middle of the diagonal line and drag down until the water darkens the right amount. Don't adjust the curves so much that the water turns totally black; it should retain enough color variety that the shadows and ripples can still be seen (Figure IV.A.4).

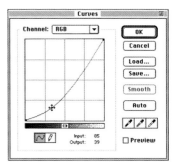

Figure IV.A.3
The Curves dialog box can be used to adjust the tonal range of an image while keeping other values constant.

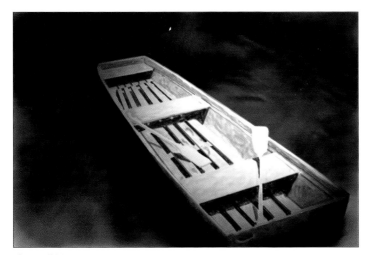

Figure IV.A.4
Darkening the water changes the painting's atmosphere to nighttime.

Change the atmosphere to a fall feel

Reopen your original painting of the boat on the pond. Save another version so that you can change the season from summer to fall.

Load the selection of the boat, then choose **Select➡Inverse** to make the water the active selection. Choose **Image➡Adjust➡ Curves**. When the Curves dialog box opens, change the Channel from RGB to Red by clicking the arrow of the box and choosing Red from the drop-down menu. Click the diagonal line and drag up to increase the red colors as shown in Figure IV.A.5.

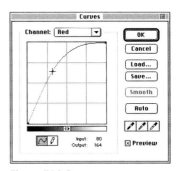

Figure IV.A.5
You can isolate the Red channel, leaving Green and Blue alone.

Changing the tonal curve of just the Red channel produces dramatic results; the greens all change to a rich, reddish color, and other values such as contrast and brightness remain the same. This creates the illusion of red and orange leaves reflecting into the pond. As you can see in Figure IV.A.6, the color of the sky changes from a greenish blue to a more purple blue—it feels like the temperature has dropped.

Figure IV.A.6
The atmosphere of the painting has been changed to that of a cool, fall afternoon.

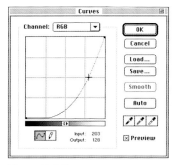

Figure IV.A.7
Alter the RGB curve to darken the boat.

Because the light on a fall afternoon is weaker than that of a summer day, the boat now appears too brightly lit. Load the boat's selection, and open the Curves dialog box once again. Click the middle of the diagonal line and drag downwards as shown in Figure IV.A.7. This darkens the boat, making it appear to be in a weaker light (Figure IV.A.8).

Figure IV.A.8
The boat is darkened to represent the weaker light of fall.

The pink tones in the water at the bottom of the picture appear unrealistic and gaudy, but they're easy to tone down. Change the foreground color to a light brown, and switch to the Paintbrush by pressing **B**. Choose the 200-pixel diameter, soft-edged brush. Press the **Return** key (Macintosh) or **Enter** key (Windows) to bring the Paintbrush Options palette to the front. Set Opacity to 40% and change the Blending mode to Color, which will have the effect of changing the color—but not brightness or contrast— as you paint over the pink areas to tone them down (Figure IV.A.9).

Figure IV.A.9
When you paint in the Color Mode, only the color changes; other values are left the same.

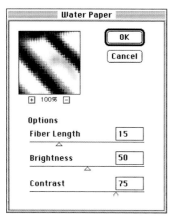

Figure IV.A.10
When applying the Water Paper filter, consult the preview box to judge the effect of various settings before clicking OK.

Add the texture of watercolor paper

You can make your painting appear to have been laid down on rough-textured watercolor paper by using the Sketch filter called Water Paper. Using this filter "absorbs" some of the paint strokes and accentuates others. Even if you intend to print your painting on real watercolor paper, the results achieved by a CMYK printing process, such as the IRIS, will not yield a hand-painted look. In this printing process, the ink is sprayed on the paper's surface evenly, and there will be no sign of areas where the paper fibers have resisted the paint as they would in traditional watercolor. That's why the Sketch filter is important; it can add back the "texture" lost in digital painting techniques.

First, load the selection of just the boat, and open the filter by choosing **Filter➧Sketch➧Water Paper**. When the Water Paper dialog box appears, it will take a few moments for the preview to update to the current settings. Wait for this to happen, and then adjust the settings. Again, you'll probably have to wait a few moments more to see how altering the settings changes the image. Because the colors in the boat are lighter than the surrounding water, we used a lower Brightness setting (50%) for the example (Figure IV.A.10).

Next, choose **Select➧Inverse** to make the water the active selection. Open the Water Paper filter again, and adjust the Brightness level upwards because the water is darker than the boat. This example used a Brightness setting of 70%. Click the sample image and use the resulting grabber hand to scroll to a view of the water. Wait for the preview to update. When you are satisfied with the effect, click **OK** and the filter will be applied (Figure IV.A.11).

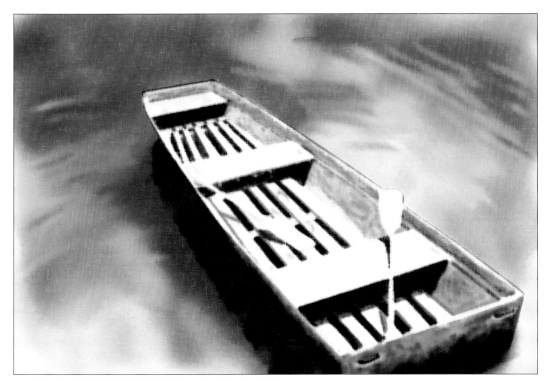

Figure IV.A.11
After you've applied the Water Paper filter, the painting takes on the texture of rough paper.

These are just a few of the many filters and effects that you can use to alter your painting. There are almost a hundred filters that come with Photoshop, organized in categories such as Artistic, Blur, Brush Strokes, Distort, Noise, Pixelate, Render, Sharpen, Sketch, Stylize, Texture, Video and Other. You can do everything from creating 3D effects to adding lens flares. You can adjust colors, blur or sharpen images, heighten or reduce contrast, and change your paintings in an almost endless variety of ways.

Spend some time exploring other filters and effects to gain more creative power than you ever imagined possible. When you want to prepare your file for final output, save it as a TIFF in CMYK mode.

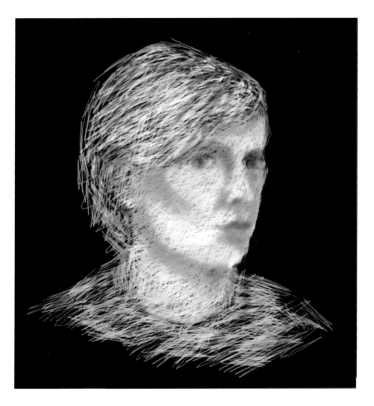

Part IV: Lesson B **Using "scratchboard" technique**

Scratchboard art has always been popular and is now becoming even more widely used. Traditionally, you needed a scratchboard or scraperboard, which is a soft, white board coated with usually black ink. The technique involved using sharp drawing tools to cut through the black layer and reveal the white underneath. A final scratchboard composition can look like a wood engraving or photo negative.

Art concepts

Scratchboard

Subtractive process

Form

Contrast

Photoshop tools and features

Eraser tool

Layers

You can emulate the scratchboard effect in Photoshop by adding a black layer to a pre-existing painting and using the Eraser tool to reveal the layer below. The digital results can be more interesting and colorful than the those with the traditional technique because you can use full color in the layer underneath, and apply the Eraser with varying Opacity levels.

This lesson uses the self-portrait pastel drawing to demonstrate the effect, but you can use any drawing or painting for this exercise. You can also create an original composition by laying down a base layer of white or color and erasing the layer above it to build up your image stroke by stroke.

Prepare the base layer

First, open the drawing or painting you want to use for this lesson. Because the complexity of the scratchboard technique is caused by the variety of strokes you make with the Eraser tool, you might want to simplify the colors and details of the painting underneath. Otherwise, the composition may become too "busy" with too many competing details.

An easy way to simplify a complex painting or drawing is to posterize it, or reduce it to a set number of colors. You can do this by choosing **Image➡Map➡Posterize**. Enter a value of less than 10 to reduce the number of colors. The example shown in Figure IV.B.1 uses just 7 levels.

Next, apply a blur to remove more detail. Choose **Filter➡Blur➡Gaussian Blur**, and enter a value of 2 or 3 pixels. Figure IV.B.1 has a 2-pixel Gaussian Blur.

Figure IV.B.1
Reduce detail and complexity in the original illustration or painting to prepare for the scratchboard technique.

Make a new layer and fill it with a solid color

Create a new layer and fill it with a solid color. This example uses black because that is a traditional scratchboard color, but you can use white, or any other color.

Use the Eraser tool to reveal the base layer

With your base image prepared, you're ready to reveal it. If you're using the self-portrait, begin your eraser strokes in the hair because it's an ideal area to develop this technique. Press **E** to change to the Eraser tool. Use the Eraser Tool Options palette to set opacity, type of brush, and whether or not to fade. You can choose the size of brush from the Brushes palette. Temporarily reduce the opacity of the solid color layer to 70% so you can see the drawing underneath, and then begin to erase the layer of solid color. Figure IV.B.2 shows the first strokes using a hard-edged 3-pixel diameter brush, with 60% Opacity, and other strokes set to fade at 20, 30, and 40 steps.

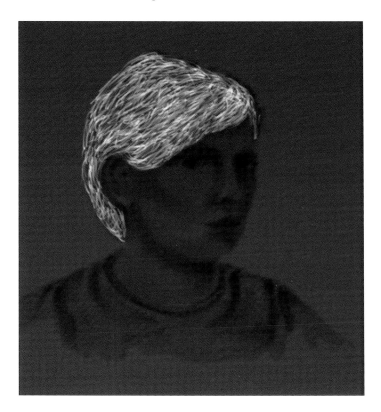

Figure IV.B.2
Begin to reveal the base drawing by erasing the layer above it.

Continue to reveal the base layer

As you develop your scratchboard painting, adjust your Eraser tool settings. Also pay attention to the direction of your strokes, subtracting in a pattern of hatching and crosshatching. You can leave more of the solid color layer in some areas to suggest shading, while other areas can be more heavily erased to create highlights.

If you're working on a portrait, such as this example, you'll probably want to erase most of the top layer that covers skin tones, but you can leave more of the solid color covering clothing, hair, and backgrounds (see Figure IV.B.3).

Figure IV.B.3
Erase the solid color until you have revealed just the right amount of your base layer.

Scratchboard compositions, particularly when done in black and white, are popular for newspaper, book, and magazine illustrations because they are so easy to reproduce.

The possibilities a scratchboard offers for the artist to juxtapose different patterns and create tonal variation make it very versatile for all kinds of art, from landscapes to still lifes, portraitures to figure work. You can also achieve levels of control and subtlety with digital scratchboard techniques that are not possible in the traditional medium.

Part IV: Lesson C   **Rendering in Impressionist style**

You can add variety to your paintings in an infinite number of ways, and Photoshop can help you. In this lesson, you'll change your airbrushed painting of the lemons and mug into an even softer, impressionist painting.

Art concepts

Impressionism

Naturalism

Pigment

Complementary color

Simultaneous contrast

Photoshop tools and features

Rubber Stamp tool

Smudge tool

Toning tools

In the impressionist style, form is more important than subject matter, with the natural appearance of objects less of a concern than the total impact of the composition. There is a notable emphasis on light and atmosphere. Artists painting in this style will often use areas of complementary colors next to each other for greater brilliance, and often apply paint heavily so that light will reflect from the actual surface of the painting. These dabs of pigment are sometimes comprised of complementary colors, and when seen from a distance, the colors form fused tones.

Because of the bright surfaces and complex shadows in the lemons and mug painting, it lends itself well to an interpretation in the impressionist style. As you go through this exercise, the silhouettes of the lemons, mug, and background will become blended together and lose their well-defined edges. As this happens, focus on the color and form and notice how the composition takes on a new liveliness.

Prepare the lemons/mug painting

Open the Part III, Lesson 3 drawing. Then select **File➡Save As**, and give the new file a different name than the original.

Begin softening the painting

To start the composition's transformation to an impressionist painting, choose the Rubber Stamp tool by pressing **S**. On the Rubber Stamp Options palette, set Opacity at 20% and Mode to Impressionist. Select a 100-pixel diameter, soft-edged brush tip.

Now start to soften the edges of the mug by dragging the Rubber Stamp over its outline. The first time you click down with the Rubber Stamp, you'll see a dialog box advising you that the Photoshop Format is being read. Wait for this process to complete, and then make short strokes along the edge of the mug. The colors of the mug and background will be blended together in a random fashion. With this large brush and low Opacity setting, you get a feel for the Impressionist effect gradually (see Figure IV.C.1).

Figure IV.C.1
Use the Rubber Stamp tool in Impressionist mode and begin "loosening up" the hard edges in your painting.

Soften the lemons

After you become more familiar with using the Rubber Stamp in Impressionist mode along the mug's edges, proceed to the edges of the lemons. Keep the settings the same as before, and notice the different effect when you stroke from the lemon into the shadow, as opposed to when you stroke from the shadow into the lemon. Continue until you have worked your way around the outline of all the lemons, as seen in Figure IV.C.2.

Figure IV.C.2
Continue to soften the entire painting by using the Rubber Stamp around the edges of all the lemons.

Use smaller, more opaque strokes

Change to a 65-pixel diameter soft-edged brush tip, and increase the Rubber Stamp's Opacity to 40%. Continue to make short strokes along the outside edges of the objects, as well as inside the lemons themselves, the mug, and the shadows.

As you apply more strokes, decrease the size of the brush and increase the opacity, until you're working with a 35-pixel diameter brush and 90% Opacity. As your brush gets smaller and the effect becomes more pronounced, make shorter strokes at similar angles. Don't make the strokes perfectly horizontal or vertical; angled ones will look better. (Figure IV.C.3)

You can use the Smudge tool to smooth edges that become too fuzzy or distorted. Finally, use the Toning (Dodge/Burn) tools to lighten or darken portions of elements that have become blended together too much. For example, two lemons may have been blurred to the point where they've lost contrast against one another. You can load the selection of one and lighten it with the Dodge tool so that it stands out against the lemon behind it. Or you can invert that selection and darken the lemon behind it with the Burn tool.

A painting in the impressionist style does not attempt a realistic depiction of light, shadow, and form. Rather, it takes greater liberty with these and other elements to create a much different feeling.

You can use the Rubber Stamp in Impressionist mode on photographs, paintings, and illustrations to achieve a diffused, stylized look. As always, carefully laid down strokes of different sizes and levels of opacity will yield a more hand-painted look than if you simply take an image and apply a filter.

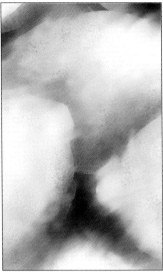

Figure IV.C.3
Make angled strokes with smaller brushes.

Part IV: Lesson D   Creating a surrealistic painting

Engaging the viewer and eliciting an emotional response is one of the goals of fine art. You can achieve this by telling stories with your paintings and by creating a provocative atmosphere or mood. Often, juxtaposing a sense of reality

Art concepts

Surrealism

Transparency

Distortion

Dimension

Perspective

Photoshop tools and features

Channels

Paths

Airbrush tool

Lasso tool

Gradient tool

Noise filter

Blur filter

Hue & Saturation

Transform

with something that would be impossible in the real world is an effective way to tell a story and reach your viewer.

Surrealism is a style of artistic expression that merges reality and fantasy, and its subjects are often experiences revealed by the subconscious. Salvador Dali, one of the most prominent surrealist painters, used a meticulous, naturalistic style that made his improbable, weird, and shocking images seem authentic.

In this lesson, you'll place your drawing of a door in a surreal context. The example image moves the door into deep space and suggests a dreamlike, light-filled world behind it. You can follow this theme, or place your door against any background you can imagine and paint. You can make an interesting contrast against the background of an ocean, a forest, or a bright afternoon sky. As you paint, try to tap into your subconscious and create an image that provokes your viewer.

Make a background of stars

Create a new Grayscale file, at 300dpi. Make the canvas large enough to contain your door and surround it with enough space to add other elements. Use Photoshop's default colors (black foreground, white background), and fill the background with 100% black.

Now, create the stars:

1. Press **M** for the Marquee tool, and draw a selection about two inches square. Choose **Filter➡Noise➡Add Noise**. Set the Amount at 200, and click **OK**.

2. Choose **Filter➡Fade Noise**, change the mode to Dissolve, and click **OK**.

3. Select **Layer➡Transform➡Scale**, and drag on the handles of the selection until it fills the entire background. Press **Return** (Macintosh) or **Enter** (Windows).

4. Make some of the white specks less visible by reducing the contrast. Choose **Image➡Adjust➡Brightness/Contrast**, and move the Contrast slider to the left. Click **OK**.

5. Choose **Filter➡Blur➡Gaussian Blur**, set the Radius at 1 or 2 pixels, and click **OK**.

You may want to adjust the brightness and contrast again, this time increasing contrast to make the stars appear brighter (Figure IV.D.1).

Change to RGB mode and color the sky

Choose **Image➡Mode➡RGB** to work in color. Change the foreground color to a deep blue-black, and then select **Edit➡Fill**. Set the Fill palette to Foreground Color, 100% Opacity, and Screen mode. When you click **OK**, the black will be replaced with blue, but the stars will not be filled.

Switch to the Airbrush tool by pressing **A**. On the Airbrush Options palette, set Pressure at 50% and Mode to Dissolve. With a 200-pixel diameter soft-edged brush tip, make several broad, curved strokes across the canvas so that some areas of the white specks are obscured. (Figure IV.D.2)

Figure IV.D.1
Create a background of stars in Grayscale mode with the Noise filter.

Figure IV.D.2
Color the sky and use the Airbrush to obscure some of the stars.

157

Figure IV.D.3
Use the Transform feature to add perspective to the door.

Make a new layer and import the door

Open the working file for your original door drawing, and position it near your new image window. Click the door's image in the Layers palette and drag the layer into the new image window. The door will automatically appear on a new layer on top of the starry background.

Make the door an active selection again, and if you want to change the side the doorknob is on, choose **Layer➡Transform➡Flip Horizontal**. Then choose **Layer➡Transform➡Perspective**, and drag one of the corner handles to make the door appear to be standing open as in Figure IV.D.3. Most likely it will appear too wide; choose **Layer➡Transform➡Distort**, and drag one of the handles on the side to make the door more narrow. Then click the door, and drag to adjust its position on the layer. Press **Return** (Macintosh) or **Enter** (Windows) to apply the transformations.

After you change the door's perspective, you need to add an edge to show the thickness of the door. Use the Pen tool to outline the edge, make the path an active selection, and add a linear gradient fill with a light gray foreground color and dark gray background.

To colorize the door's surface, choose **Image➡Adjust➡Hue/Saturation**. When the palette opens, check Colorize, and use the sliders to adjust the hue, increase saturation, and lower the brightness until you see the color you want on the door. Click **OK**.

You also need to redraw the door handle to make it appear more dimensional. You can zoom in to a high level of magnification and use the Lasso tool to outline the new handle. Then use the Paintbrush tool with a variety of small brush tip sizes to fill the outline and add detail.

Create a glow behind the door

Follow these steps to create a glow behind the door:

1. Make a new layer named *Glow* and move it underneath the door layer. Switch to the Marquee tool by pressing **M**, and draw a rectangular marquee the size of the imaginary door frame.

2. Change foreground color to yellow, and press **G** to open the Gradient tool. Fill the selection with a linear gradient by dragging from top to bottom.

3. Isolate the border by choosing **Select➡Modify➡Border**, and set the border at 36 pixels. Then choose **Select➡Feather**, and set the Feather to 12 pixels. Fill the new selection with the same yellow to white gradient (Figure IV.D.4).

Figure IV.D.4
Fill a rectangle with a yellow-to-white gradient, and then select and feather its border and fill again.

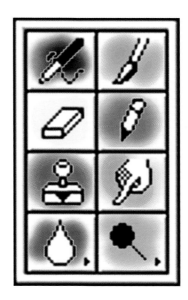

Part V: The Photoshop paintbox

Creating fine art in Photoshop is more rewarding if you've mastered the core set of painting and drawing tools—Pencil, Paintbrush, Airbrush, Eraser, Rubber Stamp, Smudge, Focus (Blur and Sharpen), and Toning (Dodge, Burn, and Sponge)—those we call the Photoshop paintbox. Because we assume you have a basic knowledge of Photoshop, and already know how to use simple tools such as the Marquee or Magic Wand tools, we will limit our review in this section to the paintbox tools. Other tools such as Gradient, Pen, and Paint Bucket are discussed in the lessons. Check the index for the page references.

This section is meant to jump-start your creativity by visually linking settings on different palettes to their results. Study the examples shown to find approaches that will best serve your artistic goals. Don't be afraid to experiment and try variations on the settings we suggest. Add to our collection by making your own thumbnails of techniques and arranging them so that you can note the settings for future reference. Print them out and keep them together with this book.

As you progress, learn the keyboard shortcuts for these tools so that you can work quickly and with fewer open windows. This can be a real plus if you're working on a small monitor. While you're painting or drawing, keep the Navigator palette open. It will help you to move through your image easily and help you avoid getting lost when you zoom in for detail work.

The paintbox tools

The painting and drawing tools shown here comprise the Photoshop paintbox. The keyboard shortcuts for the tools are in parentheses. Select hidden tools Sharpen, Burn, and Sponge by dragging, or Option-clicking (Macintosh) or Alt-clicking (Windows) on the toolbox icon.

Each tool has Stylus Pressure settings. These are only available if you have a properly-installed graphics tablet such as the Wacom or Calcomp tablets.

The **Airbrush** tool creates soft-edged strokes. Settings include Pressure, Painting Mode, Fade to Transparent or Background, and Stylus Pressure.

*Airbrush (**A**)*

The **Paintbrush** tool paints hard-edged or soft-edged anti-aliased strokes. Settings include Opacity, Painting Mode, Fade to Transparent or Background, Wet Edges, and Stylus Pressure.

*Paintbrush (**B**)*

The **Eraser** tool deletes pixels and restores parts of saved images. Settings include Erasing Mode, Opacity, Fade, Erase Image, Erase to Saved, Wet Edges, and Stylus Pressure.

*Eraser (**E**)*

The **Pencil** tool draws hard-edged strokes (jaggies visible). Settings include Opacity, Painting Mode, Fade to Transparent or Background, Auto-erase, and Stylus Pressure.

*Pencil (**Y**)*

The **Rubber Stamp** tool copies parts of an image. Settings include Cloning Method, Effect Mode, Opacity, Sample Merged, and Stylus Pressure.

*Rubber Stamp (**S**)*

The **Smudge** tool mixes color in an image area. Settings include Effect Mode, Pressure, Finger Painting, Sample Merged, and Stylus Pressure.

*Smudge (**U**)*

The **Focus** tools blur or sharpen edges. Settings include Tool Choice, Effect Mode, Pressure, Sample Merged, and Stylus Pressure. Press **R** to cycle between Blur and Sharpen.

*Focus (**R**) Blur, Sharpen*

The **Toning** tools lighten, darken, or otherwise change the color saturation of an image area. Settings include Tool Choice and Operations, Exposure, and Stylus Pressure. Press **O** to cycle among Dodge, Burn and Sponge.

*Toning (**O**) Dodge, Burn, Sponge*

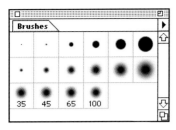

Brushes Palette

You must make a selection from the Brushes palette whenever using any of the eight painting and editing tools in the Photoshop paintbox. When you choose a brush setting for a particular tool, it applies only to that tool. For example, you might select a 2-pixel, hard-edged brush for the Paintbrush tool and a 35-pixel, soft-edged brush for the Airbrush tool. As you switch back and forth from the Paintbrush to the Airbrush, the selection displayed by the Brushes palette will change. Using this palette, you can also create, delete, and define brushes, as well as reset, load, replace, and save sets of brushes.

Choosing brush style and size

To select a brush for a tool, first choose the tool you want to use, then select **Window➛Show Brushes** or press **F5**. When the Brushes palette displays, click the brush of your choice.

Creating new brushes

There are two methods for creating a new brush: modifying an existing brush and adding a new brush shape.

Modifying a brush shape

To edit a brush, select a brush shape and double-click that brush in Brushes palette. The Brush Options dialog box opens. Change the settings for diameter, hardness, spacing, angle, and roundness, which are displayed in the square on the bottom right. Click OK to accept the changes to the brush shape.

Pull-down menu found on the Brushes palette

Adding a new brush shape

To add a new brush to your palette double-click an empty brush shape slot or choose New Brush from the top right pull-down menu. The dialog box title bar reads New Brush Options, but the variables are the same as for modifying a brush shape. Click OK to add the new brush shape to the palette.

Brush Options

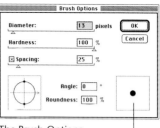

The Brush Options
dialog box

Brush changes displayed here

Setting diameter, hardness, and spacing values

To change brush diameter (measured in pixels), hardness, or spacing enter a number value or drag the slider to set the brush option.

The size of a brush shape's hard center scales from 100% (hardest) to 0% (softest) and is measured as a percentage of the brush diameter. If the number is 45%, the brush shape has a hard center that's less than half the total brush width.

The spacing option changes the distance between the stroke's brush marks. At 100% each brush mark will just touch each other. The closer the value is to 0%, the more each brush mark will overlap. The greater the number above 100%, the further apart the brush marks paint.

Angling your brush stroke

You can create calligraphic effects with elliptical brushes. Enter a value from 0° to 360° as either plus or minus degrees (45° or −45°), or drag the horizontal axis in the left preview box.

Changing brush tip shapes

Type a value or drag the points in the Brush Options' left preview box. Decreasing the value reduces the diameter on one axis changing the brush shape from a circle (100%) to an ellipse (1-99%) to a linear brush (0%).

Deleting a brush shape

Press **Command** (Macintosh) or **Ctrl** (Windows) to display the Scissors cursor, then click on a brush shape to remove it from the Brushes palette.

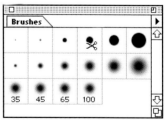

Deleting a brush shape

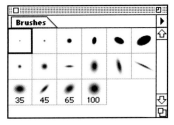

A new set of brushes

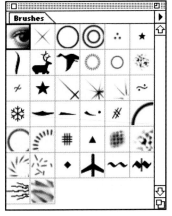

Assorted brushes

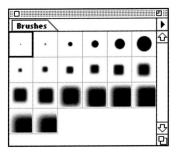

Drop Shadow brushes

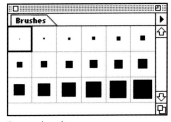

Square brushes

Creating a brush library

As you develop your brush skills, you may want to create and save sets of brushes for achieving various effects. For instance, a set could be made of the same size and shape brush with copies at numerous different angles. When painting with a set such as this you could quickly cycle through the choices by pressing [or] (left or right bracket) and by doing so avoid the monotonous, programmed look of all brush strokes at the same angle. After you make a set of brushes, save them (use a descriptive name) in the program's Brushes & Patterns folder by choosing Save Brushes from the pull-down menu.

Additional Photoshop Brush Sets

There are three additional Photoshop brush sets: Assorted, Drop Shadow and Square Brushes. Square Brushes offers an anti-aliased option. Anti-aliasing is not available for some of the brushes in the Assorted or Drop Shadow set, the bottom two rows in Drop Shadow for example.

These additional brush sets are found in Photoshop's Goodies folder. You can add them to your Brushes palette by choosing Load Brushes or Replace Brushes from the pallette menu.

Using the Pencil

The Pencil tool draws hard-edged strokes (jaggies visible).

Selecting the Pencil

To choose the Pencil tool, press **Y**. Double-click the Pencil icon to open the Pencil Options palette. Options include Opacity, Painting Mode, Fade to Transparent or Background, Auto-erase, and Stylus Pressure.

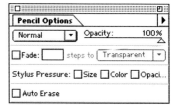

Pencil Options palette

Changing the pencil point quickly

Press either **[** or **]** (left or right brackets) to cycle through the choices in the Brushes palette.

Constraining pencil strokes

The pencil strokes here were made using selections from the first row of nibs in the Brushes palette. They display the jagged edges characteristic of this tool, which does not use anti-aliasing. The setting is Normal, Opacity is 100%, and Fade, Stylus Pressure, and Wet Edges are not selected. Make constrained pencil strokes by clicking where you want the stroke to begin, holding the Shift key down and clicking at the endpoint. The horizontal strokes are a 2-pixel Pencil; vertical are 13-pixel.

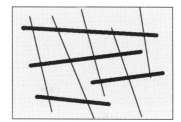

Making freehand pencil strokes

These strokes were made without using the Shift key to constrain the lines. The lighter strokes are made with a 5-pixel Pencil, the heavier ones with a 45-pixel Pencil. The other settings are Normal, Opacity at 100%, and Fade, Stylus Pressure and Wet Edges are unselected.

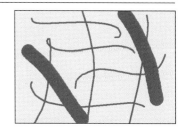

Making semi-transparent pencil strokes

You can make strokes more transparent with the Opacity slider. The example here is at 40% Opacity. Type 4 to easily change the Opacity slider to 40%. Typing 1 will set it to 10%, 0 to 100%. Notice how the color darkens by building up where the strokes cross over each other.

169

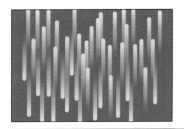

Making pencil strokes fade to transparency

This example uses a 5-pixel Pencil, with Fade to Transparency at 45 steps. The lines are constrained, and some of them are drawn from top to bottom, the others from bottom to top. Increasing the number of steps for the fade produces longer lines.

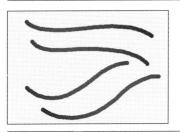

Making pencil strokes fade to a color

Select a background color for fading, and enter the number of steps for Fade to Background. The fade will be earlier in the line for fewer steps, later in the line for more. This example uses a 13-pixel Pencil, with Fade to Background at 100 steps.

Using the pencil with a graphics tablet

If you have a graphics tablet and the proper software installed, you can vary Pencil Size, Color, and Opacity with stylus pressure. The variety you can achieve by varying pressure is shown in these three examples.

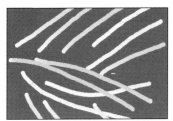

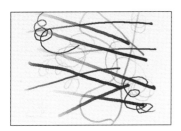

Using the Paintbrush

The Paintbrush makes softer, anti-aliased strokes.

Selecting the Paintbrush

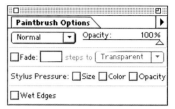

To choose the Paintbrush tool, press **B**. Double-click the Paintbrush icon to open the Paintbrush Options palette. Options include Opacity, Painting Mode, Fade to Transparent or Background, Wet Edges, and Stylus Pressure.

Changing the brush shape quickly

Press either **[** or **]** (left or right brackets) to cycle through the choices in the Brushes palette.

Making constrained brushstrokes

Brush strokes are constrained by clicking where you want the stroke to begin, holding the Shift key down, and clicking at the endpoint. The strokes shown in this example were made with selections from the first row in the Brushes palette. The setting is Normal, Opacity is at 100%, and Fade, Stylus Pressure, and Wet Edges are not selected.

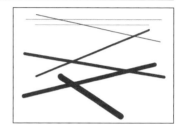

Making soft-edged brush strokes

By selecting softer-edged brushes from the second or third row of the Brushes palette, you can achieve edges that blend into the background, such as those shown here. This can give brush strokes a more realistic appearance.

Making semi-transparent brush strokes

You can change opacity by using the slider or typing the first number of the percentage you want. The brush strokes shown here are white, with 40% Opacity. Notice how the lines lighten progressively as they cross over one another, which adds an illusion of depth to the image.

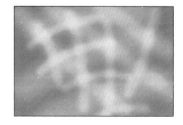

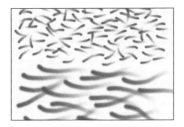

Making brush strokes fade to transparent

These strokes were made by selecting the Fade option and specifying a number of steps for Fade to Transparent. The short strokes on top are set to fade at 20 steps, those on the bottom at 40. The number of steps you select will determine the length of your strokes.

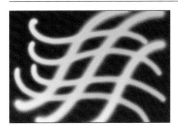

Making brush strokes fade to another color

By selecting a new background color and Fade to Background, you can achieve this kind of effect. These strokes were made with large, soft-edged brushes and a 20-step fade.

Making brush strokes with wet edges

When you choose the Wet Edges feature on the Brushes palette, you can add a watercolor effect where the paint builds up along the outside edges of the brush stroke, as shown here. Notice how the effect multiplies when the strokes cross over one another because the brush has become more transparent in the center.

Using the paintbrush with a graphics tablet

If you have a drawing tablet such as the Calcomp Ultra Slate, you can vary Brush Size, Color, and Opacity with stylus pressure. The variety you can achieve by varying pressure is shown in these three examples.

Variations with the Brush Options palette

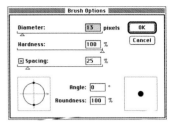

When you double-click a brush in the Brushes palette or select Brush Options from the palette's pull-down menu, you open the Brush Options sub-palette. By changing these settings, you can vary the diameter, hardness, spacing, angle, and roundness of any brush. The first example shown here illustrates variation in brush hardness from 0 on top, to 25%, 50%, and 75% on the bottom.

Brush Options sub-palette

The second example shows the effect of different spacing settings, left to right, 25%, 50%, 100%, and 200%. Be careful when changing these settings, however, because the mathematically-derived spacing effect can give a mechanistic, computer-driven appearance to your artwork.

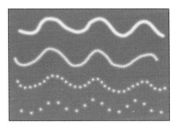

The last example illustrates the calligraphic effect you can achieve by changing the roundness of a brush, and then changing the angle. It uses a large brush with 10% roundness, and strokes at varying angles.

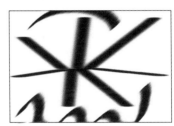

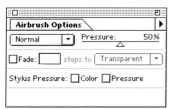

Airbrush Options palette

Using the Airbrush

The Airbrush tool creates diffused, soft-edged strokes whose intensity increases with pressure applied.

Selecting the Airbrush

To choose the Airbrush tool, press **A**. Double-click the Airbrush icon to open the Airbrush Options palette. Options include Pressure, Painting Mode, Fade to Transparent or Background, and Stylus Pressure.

Changing the brush shape quickly

Type either **[** or **]** (left or right brackets) to cycle through the choices in the Brushes palette.

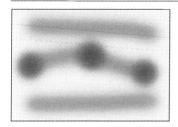

Regulating pressure with the Airbrush

The Airbrush tool works in a similar fashion to a traditional airbrush, meaning that you can determine how quickly a spray of paint is applied by changing the pressure setting. You can apply gradual tones with more diffuse edges than those of the Paintbrush. Pressing the mouse button builds up the color; the pressure setting determines how quickly the color builds. In the example shown here, the Opacity is 25% and a 100-pixel, soft-edged brush is used. The strokes on the top and bottom were made by quickly passing the mouse over the image with the button clicked; the stroke in the middle shows the effect of pausing to let the color build in three locations while painting the stroke.

Making Airbrush strokes fade to transparent

When you select Fade on the Airbrush Options palette, enter a number of steps, and choose Transparent, you can achieve effects like the ones seen in this example. These are constrained strokes, with 50% Pressure and a 30-step fade. Notice how the fade is slower with the large 100-pixel brush on top, and happens more quickly as the brush gets smaller. Don't confuse the Pressure setting on the Airbrush Options palette with the Opacity setting on the Paintbrush Options palette; the strokes laid down by the airbrush at 50% Pressure are not 50% transparent, and therefore tend to cover over the strokes beneath them.

Making Airbrush strokes fade to a color

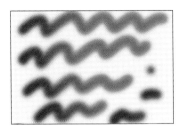

Select a new background color, and change the Fade to background if you want the airbrush stroke to fade to another color. This example uses a 45-pixel soft-edged brush, 60% Pressure, and 20-step fade. You can see that the distance of dark brown laid down is always the same, while the length of the lighter brown is dependent on the length of the stroke.

Using the Airbrush with a graphics tablet

With a graphics tablet, you can create color and pressure variations in airbrush strokes. The first example here shows variations in color from pressure; the second shows variations in pressure itself. Unlike the Paintbrush or Pencil, no option is available for linking stroke size to the stylus pressure. Using stylus pressure to vary Airbrush tool effects gives a more realistic look to your work because the fading is artist-controlled, not determined by a number of steps.

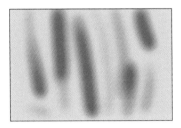

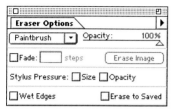

Eraser Options palette

Using the Eraser

The Eraser tool deletes pixels and restores parts of saved images.

Selecting the Eraser

To choose the Eraser tool, press **E**. Double-click the Eraser icon to open the Eraser Options palette. Options include Opacity, Erasing Mode, Fade to Transparent or Background, Erase Image, Erase to Saved, Wet Edges, and Stylus Pressure.

Changing the brush shape quickly

Type either **[** or **]** (left or right brackets) to cycle through the choices in the Brushes palette (except block erasing mode).

Changing the shape of the Eraser

Choose any of four shapes for the Eraser: Paintbrush, Airbrush, Pencil, or Block. This example shows results of erasing the dark gray to a light green background, the Paintbrush on the top, Airbrush on the right, Pencil on the bottom, and Block on the left. Unless using the Block, you must choose a brush from the Brushes palette to define the size and shape of your Eraser. The Block will always erase at the same size from any level of magnification. When your view is zoomed in, it will erase a smaller portion of your image than when your view is zoomed out.

Changing the transparency of the Eraser

When erasing with the Paintbrush, Airbrush, or Pencil, you can get the effect of erasing very lightly by lowering the opacity level of the tool. The example here illustrates various levels of transparency for each of these three settings. The Paintbrush is erasing the light colored rectangle on the top edge, the Airbrush on the right, and the Pencil on the bottom.

Changing the fade of the Eraser

With the Paintbrush, Airbrush, or Pencil chosen for the Eraser tool you can set levels of Fade to Transparency. The example here shows a 20-step fade with the Paintbrush on top, the Airbrush on the right, and the Pencil on the bottom. Fading is not available in Block mode.

Using the Eraser with a graphics tablet

With a graphics tablet, you can choose to vary Eraser Size or Opacity with the pressure of your stylus. The first example shows variation in Pressure for the Paintbrush, Airbrush, and Pencil modes of the Eraser tool. The second shows variation in Opacity with Stylus Pressure.

Erasing with Wet Edges

If you are using the Paintbrush mode to erase, you can select Wet Edges on the Eraser Options palette to get the watercolor effect seen here. This example uses a 5-pixel brush on the top at 60% Opacity, a 17-pixel brush on the right side with 60% Opacity, and a 17-pixel brush on the bottom at 100% Opacity.

Erasing to a previously-saved version

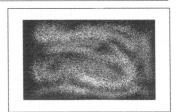

With this option, you can erase back to a version you've previously saved. Being able to do this gives you a way to combine several effects. For the first example shown here, a rectangle was filled in a solid brown and sprayed with an Airbrush in two lighter colors, using Dissolve mode. The file was then saved. The rectangle was filled solid brown and worked back with an Eraser, as shown in the second example. Erase to Saved was selected, and the Eraser is in Airbrush mode with a 30% Opacity level. This filters the rather harsh dissolve pixels and adds depth and complexity to the composition.

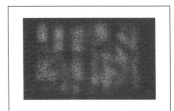

Using the Rubber Stamp

The Rubber Stamp tool copies parts of an image to another area.

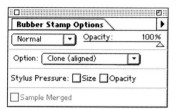

Rubber Stamp Options palette

Selecting the Rubber Stamp

To choose the Rubber Stamp tool, press **S**. Double-click the Rubber Stamp icon to open the Rubber Stamp Options palette. Options include Opacity, Effect Mode, Cloning Methods, Sample Merged, and Stylus Pressure.

Changing the brush shape quickly

Type either **[** or **]** (left or right brackets) to cycle through the choices in the Brushes palette.

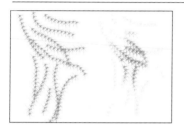

Stamping with varying opacity

Changing the Opacity level of the Rubber Stamp allows a gradual buildup of an image. The example here shows the original image on the left. After Option-clicking (Macintosh) or Alt-clicking (Windows) the original image, a clone is gradually built up on the right side using a large, soft-edged brush with Opacity set to 30%. This example uses the Clone (aligned) option, which means all strokes laid down after the first one maintain the correct relative distance from it. The areas in the center where the clone is darker are produced by painting over with additional brush strokes.

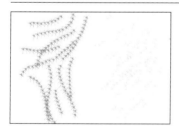

Stamping with Clone (non-aligned)

When you choose Clone (non-aligned), each time you click the mouse while making the clone, you get a stroke that begins at the center of the pickup location. The example here shows how this method builds up strokes. Like the preceding example, it uses a 30% opacity level, and a large, soft-edged brush.

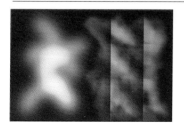

Stamping with Pattern (aligned)

You create a pattern by making a rectangular selection of an image and choosing **Edit➧Define Pattern**. Here, the image on the left is the pattern, and the clone on the right is constructed by choosing Pattern aligned, and a soft-edged brush at 50% opacity. As strokes are laid down, they create tiles of the original pattern, getting heavier as they are laid over one another.

Stamping with Pattern (non-aligned)

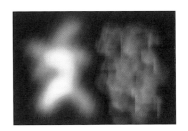

In the example shown here, a rectangle is selected from the image on the left. **Edit➡Define Pattern** makes this pattern the image laid down by the Rubber Stamp tool on the right. Notice the vertical and horizontal lines in the cloned image; each time the stamp is applied, the pattern begins again from the pickup point. Building strokes this way produces a more random pattern than the Aligned option.

Stamping From Snapshot or From Saved

These two examples illustrate how you can create an image, apply it to the Rubber Stamp, alter the image, and use the Rubber Stamp to work elements of the original back into it. After the composition on the left was saved, the color of the strokes was changed from blue to yellow, and **Edit➡Take Snapshot** chosen. Then the color change was undone, and the yellow was added back in to portions of the image with the Rubber Stamp option From Snapshot. You can do the same thing from a previously saved version of the file.

Stamping with Impressionist

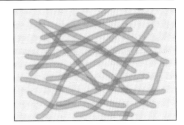

The two images here show the effect of using the Rubber Stamp in Impressionist mode. The original strokes were laid down with a medium-sized, semi-transparent brush with Wet Edges. In the second example, the Rubber Stamp in Impressionist mode is set to a large, hard-edged brush and strokes are painted over the entire surface to create the mottled colors.

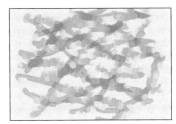

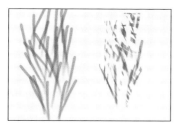

Using the Rubber Stamp with a graphics tablet

If you have a graphics tablet, you can also vary the Rubber Stamp's size and opacity by stylus pressure. In the examples here, the strokes on the lighter colored background show increasing Rubber Stamp size as more stylus pressure is applied; those on the darker background show heavier stylus pressure near the center of the clone, with lighter pressure around the edges.

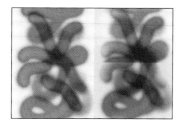

Stamping with Sample Merged

When you're working in layers, you may want to use the Rubber Stamp in Sample Merged mode. This means it will reproduce colors from all visible layers, not just the one you're working in. In this example, the original image is on the left and is comprised of brown strokes in one layer, with the lighter background in its own layer. The clone is on the right, and on top it is made with Sample Merged turned on and with Sample Merge turned off on the bottom. The option can be turned off and on after the original image has been picked up.

Using the Smudge tool

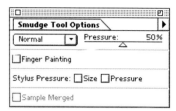

The Smudge tool blends colors by smearing the selected color into an image area.

Selecting the Smudge

To choose the Smudge tool, press **U**. Double-click the Smudge icon to open the Smudge Options palette. Options include Effect Mode, Pressure, Finger Painting, Sample Merged, and Stylus Pressure.

Smudge Tool Options palette

Changing the brush shape quickly

Type either **[** or **]** (left or right brackets) to cycle through the choices in the Brushes palette.

Changing the shape of the Smudge

Choose any existing or custom brush tip for smudging. Whichever one you apply can yield inexact or unplanned results. Make only one stroke at a time and assess its effect so you can Undo if you don't like the smudge. The smudges seen on the left of the example push the outside color into the light rectangle with a 45-pixel soft-edged brush at Opacity levels of (top to bottom) 100%, 95%, 90%, and 80%. Those on the right (top to bottom) use a 13 pixel hard-edged brush, at 30%, 40%, 50%, 60%, 70%, 80%, 90% and 100% Opacity.

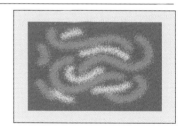

Finger painting with the Smudge

These two examples illustrate the Finger Painting mode of the Smudge tool. The first image was smudged at 50% Pressure with a 45-pixel soft-edged brush, with Finger Painting selected.

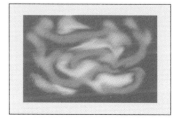

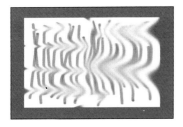

Using a graphics tablet with the Smudge

If you have a graphics tablet, you can alter Smudge Size and Pressure with the amount of pressure you apply to the stylus. The first example here shows variation in size; the smudges on the left of the image are made with less stylus pressure, whereas those on the right are made with greater pressure. The second example shows variation in smudge pressure when greater or lesser pressure is applied to the stylus. The smudges in from the top were made with greater pressure, those from the bottom up with less.

Using Sample Merged with the Smudge

If you select Sample Merged, the Smudge tool will pick up colors from visible layers other than the one you're working on. In this example, the dark red is the background layer, the second layer contains the blue rectangle, and a third layer the light red rectangle. The smudges from the top are made with Sample Merged selected and drawn down from near the border; the smudges from the bottom up are also drawn from near the border but did not affect the dark red or blue because Sample Merged was not selected.

Using the Focus tools

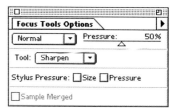

The Focus tools blur or sharpen edges between pixels.

Selecting the Focus tools

To choose the Focus tool (Blur), press **R**. Select hidden tool Sharpen by dragging, or Option-click (Macintosh) or Alt-click (Windows) the icon. Double-click the Focus icon to open the Focus Options palette. Options include Type of Tool, Effect Mode, Pressure, Sample Merged, and Stylus Pressure.

Focus Tools Options palette

Changing the brush shape quickly

Type either [or] (left or right brackets) to cycle through the choices in the Brushes palette.

Blurring or sharpening with the Focus tools

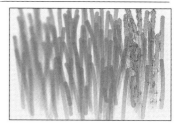

Toggle between blur and sharpen by pressing **R**, or you can change to one or the other in the Focus Tools Options palette. This example shows original strokes which were laid down with a fading paintbrush (in the center). Those on the left were blurred with the Focus tool set to 100% Opacity, and a 100-pixel soft-edged brush. Those on the right were sharpened with the same settings. Lower Opacity settings will yield more subtle results.

Using the Focus tools with a graphics tablet

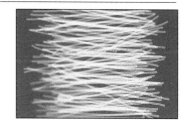

If you have a graphics tablet, you can use pressure on the stylus to increase or decrease size or opacity of your focus strokes. The example here shows use of the Blur tool with increased size as more pressure is applied near the bottom of the image. Use of the Sharpen tool with Pressure checked and more pressure is applied toward the bottom of the image.

Using Sample Merged with the Focus tools

Check Sample Merged on the Focus Tool Options palette to blur or sharpen all the visible layers in an image. Here the outside color fills the background layer, the blue rectangle is on a second layer, and the yellow rectangle is on a third. Sample Merged has been selected for the strokes made from the center to the top and bottom, and unchecked for those from the center to the sides.

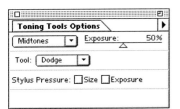

Toning Tools Options palette

Using the Toning tools

The Toning tools lighten, darken or change the color saturation of an image area.

Selecting the Toning tools

To choose the Toning tool (Dodge), press **O**. Select the hidden tools Burn and Sponge by dragging, or Opt-click (Macintosh) or Alt-click (Windows) the icon. Double-click the Toning icon to open the Toning Options palette. Options include Type of Tool, Tool Operations, Exposure, and Stylus Pressure.

Changing the brush shape quickly

Type either **[** or **]** (left or right brackets) to cycle through the choices in the Brushes palette.

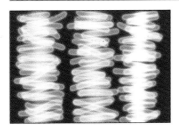

Lightening shadows, midtones, or highlights

The Dodge tool is used to lighten image areas. The example here shows lightened shadows on the left, midtones in the middle, and highlights on the right. A 100-pixel, soft-edged brush has been used at 100% Opacity for the shadows and midtones, and at 30% Opacity for the highlights.

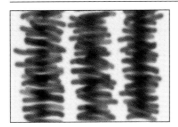

Darkening shadows, midtones or highlights

Use the Burn tool to darken image areas. Here you can see the effects of burning with a 100-pixel, soft-edged brush. On the left shadows are darkened, and in the middle midtones are darkened, both at 100% Opacity. On the right Opacity is lowered to 50%, and the same brush is used to darken the highlights.

Increasing or decreasing color

The Sponge tool is used to saturate or desaturate the color in portions of your image. The example here illustrates several strokes with the Sponge set to Saturate on the top and set to Desaturate on the bottom. The results are a heightening of the colors on top, where you can see more yellow, and a toning down of the color in the bottom, where the vertical brush strokes have become more gray.

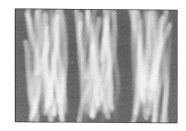

Using the toning tools with a graphics tablet

If you have a graphics tablet installed, you can alter the strokes you make with the toning tool by applying more or less stylus pressure. With the Dodge and Burn tools you can alter Size and Exposure, and with the Sponge tool you can alter Size and Pressure. The two examples shown here were created using a graphics tablet with differing stylus pressure. The first illustrates an increase in size using the Dodge tool, with more pressure as the strokes move to the right. The second shows the effects of increased pressure using the Dodge tool to lighten the colors in the center of the image, with less stylus pressure towards the outside edges.

The examples here only begin to show the wide variety of artistic expression you can achieve with the Paintbox tools. The more digital art you create, the more ways you'll discover how it can contribute to your personal style.

Part VI Printing your artwork

The growing number of service bureaus catering to artists, the increasing frequency and higher visibility of digital art exhibitions, and the financial returns some artists are reaping from their work all indicate that this is a pivotal moment in digital art. Thanks to a handful of printers who embrace new technology at the same time they honor the traditions of fine arts printmaking, electronic prints of digital images have reached new levels of quality, longevity, and legitimacy.

Why you should consider fine arts prints

If you are serious about exhibiting and marketing your artwork, you must acknowledge the standards that are being set for digital art work reproduced on paper or canvas. The traditional art businesses of museums, galleries, and art collectors are no longer ignoring digital technology.

Consider several examples of why you need to take this to heart. In the past two years such noted international artists as David Hockney and Robert Rauschenberg have exhibited IRIS prints in major New York exhibitions and sold the work for tens of thousands of dollars. Photographer Pedro Meyer had his work featured in an exhibition sponsored by Aperture, a leading publisher of fine art photography monographs. In September 1997, The Vinalhaven Press, a fine art press and workshop in Vinalhaven, Maine, that invites a few nationally or internationally known artists each summer to work with a rotating roster of master printers, cosponsored a symposium, "Media for the Next Millennium," with The McMullen Museum of Art at Boston College. At the event, guest speakers and museum print curators, who viewed demonstrations by master printers at Vinalhaven

Press, discussed the future of printmaking and the influence of new media and techniques. The symposium's announced purpose was "to assist in an examination of the impact of new technology on the traditional media of printmaking and reproduction, and to inform the wide range of individuals and practitioners involved."

What distinguishes a fine arts print?

The art world defines archival prints by drawing on the traditions of printmaking (such as etching and engraving), photography, and fine arts reproductions. In traditional printmaking, an "original print" is an impression from one or more printing plates or matrices that originated from the artist's hand and have been printed under the artist's direction in a strictly controlled edition. The edition bears the artist's signature and a description of the exact nature of the proof or edition print. When the edition is complete, the printing plates or matrices are destroyed. California and New York, sites of many professional galleries, currently have laws regulating the term "original print."

John Cone of Cone Editions and a founder of The International Association of Fine Art Digital Printmakers, drawing upon his experience as both a traditional and a high-tech fine arts printer, offers this adaptation for digital artists: "As a means of producing original prints, in computer-generated printmaking the digital image can be seen as a matrix. The array of pixels is the printing plate. The artwork may have at its source a scanned image, but the important thing is that the pixel array must be substantially by the hand of the artist—that the digital image is not merely a color-corrected version of a scanned transparency."

Such an original work of art is different from the results of converting a traditional painting or drawing into a digital file and printing it digitally using the IRIS or other wide-format ink jet printer process. Although both types of works are available as digital prints, the value of a fine arts reproduction (depending upon who the artist is) can be lower. Who purchases the work, where it is exhibited, and whether a museum will consider acquiring the work can be affected by whether or not a work is designated as an original or reproduction.

Selecting a fine art digital printmaker

Talk to as many fine art digital printmakers as you can, and judge their responsiveness, operational styles, commitment to artist clients, and ancillary services. You should look for a partner who wants to establish a long-term collaborative relationship and is interested in experimenting with computer hardware and software. Make sure they emphasize the value of personal inter-action with artists.

Also consider location. Although these specialized service bu-reaus can work across long distances, the better ones prefer that artists be on-site, especially for the first stages of proofing. When ink tables need to be calibrated to many different sheets of printmaking and artist papers, determining correct color is a matter for subjective interpretation. In Appendix A, you will find a list of fine art digital printmakers.

Preparing files

Your digital image can be stored on a floppy disk, a SyQuest cartridge, or a Zip disk. Resolution and file sizes vary consider-ably, but it's important to note that you do not necessarily need a 100 MB image to get good results. Depending on the nature of the image and the size at which it is output, files small enough to fit on a floppy disk can yield decent results. Most service bureaus are also able to scan high-resolution photographic transparencies or prints to create the digital file needed for fine art digital print-ing. In any case, begin by discussing file size, resolution, and preparation with the experts at your service bureau.

Printer options

The IRIS 3047 Graphic Printer, the leading choice of major art-ists, is a four-color, continuous-tone machine that can accurately reproduce multiple color transitions and intricate detail. The print quality competes favorably with traditional lithography and screen printing, the standards for fine arts reproduction.

IRIS ink-jet printers create images by spraying microscopic droplets from a nozzle onto a substrate that is attached to a drum rotating at 100 to 200 inches per minute. These droplets, indistinguishable to the unaided eye, build vivid, appealing surfaces at an approximate resolution of 1200 to 1800 dpi, making the IRIS print an excellent choice for reproducing hard-edged paintings, watercolors, or fine-grained photographs.

Recent advances by Encad, CalComp, and others in their field have provided other options for color output, and a list of these companies appears in Appendix A. Again, discuss different output choices with your fine art digital printmaker to find a machine whose output is the best aesthetic match for your work.

Size restrictions

IRIS prints of a reasonable digital file can be scaled from postage-stamp size to multipanel mural without significant degradation of the image. The IRIS 3047 can output individual images up to 34×46 inches, and grouping several images onto one large sheet can be an excellent way to create portfolio samples.

Because they continuously feed paper rather than wrap it around a drum such as IRIS, other printers from Encad and CalComp can print 50-inch-wide sheets several feet long. Check the corporate web sites (listed in Appendix A) for more details about individual product capabilities.

Paper choices

Most fine arts service bureaus are flexible and offer considerable variety. Nash Editions, the pioneer who introduced the fine art digital print market, discovered that Arches, Rives 640-gram cold-pressed, and Somerset Velvet art papers produce excellent results. IRIS Graphics and Encad, among others, have introduced a specially formulated canvas for ink-jet printing. Several printers have developed proprietary coatings to prepare exotic substrates for successful printing. A word of caution, however, because some of these coatings can cause the ink to fail over time. Do research first to make sure these coatings will work with your substrate and ink set. If you have a particular paper in mind, send a sample for evaluation.

Also beware of color shifts from paper to paper. Printed on a uniform glossy surface, an image appears purer and more brilliant in hue, whereas the same image on an uncoated or rough substrate looks duller. Printing on toned or off-white papers can also subdue palettes, thereby minimizing key color relationships or compositional details.

In selecting a fine arts paper, or any paper for printing your artwork to, there are tradeoffs to consider. This holds true also for deciding whether to print on paper or canvas. To begin, first look at your image. What are the important characteristics of the work? Does the content make reference to specific sensory or physical properties? Is this physical sensibility built by your use of textures or gradients? The aesthetic quality, or your enjoyment of what you see, can be dampened if the paper or canvas's surface, its overall texture, and reflective light properties do not match what your image shows. This mismatching can be the difference between your artwork looking like an art reproduction selling in discount stores and an original work of art.

Remember that your fine art digital printmaker is your partner. The printmaker is there to help you make the best selection of substrate. Take advantage of the studio's expertise and willingness to test the suitability of any unusual paper that you discover.

Archival qualities

How to Care for Works of Art on Paper, published by the Museum of Fine Arts in Boston, says, "It must be remembered that *all* light fades works of art on paper." Although a new medium, IRIS prints suffer from this same problem. Listed in Appendix A are tips for finding web sites and other resources about handling and caring for works of art. Preserving a work begins with the selection of the substrate or media on which you print.

Archival concerns often focus on the pH factor of the substrate rather than the characteristics of the pigments or dyes. Although most paper mills have adopted standards for acid-free paper, the solution for archival-quality ink-jet printing is not that simple. The value of pH-neutral papers can be lost, for instance, through application of UV coatings that help stabilize the colors of ink-jet prints.

Concerns about a print's stability have often dissuaded artists from ink-jet printing. Having developed proprietary combinations of ink sets, coatings, and stabilizers, today's fine art master printers feel they can offer good alternatives to traditional photographic prints (Appendix B contains more information about ink and media stability).

Test results have been presented by Wilhelm Imaging Research on the continuing controversy about longevity of IRIS and other ink sets at the October 1997 meeting of the International Association of Fine Art Digital Printmakers (IAFADP). Contact information for the IAFADP and other resources in Appendices A and B will help you to monitor the ongoing discussion and research efforts to solve this nagging problem for artists, printmakers, vendors, conservators, and art collectors.

Documentation of prints

Although fine art digital printers work with their artists to set the standards, authenticity and documentation can still pose problems for digital artists. Because the untrained eye might not differentiate between original computer art and a reproduction produced from a high-resolution scan, accurately documenting artwork becomes an important factor in establishing the credibility, higher prices, and collectibility that original prints command.

John Cone suggests the following details as important to document: artist, type of work, medium, image size, paper size, paper, print number, process description, additional printings or handwork (color, technique, comments), edition size, number of proofs, and pertinent dates. Such documentation should carry a statement of declaration that reads, "We attest that the above information is correct and that no other proofs or impressions exist that are not part of this documentation sheet" and be signed and dated by the printer and the artist.

Practicing good documentation and adhering to the finest standards of printing will position you as an artist whose work is taken seriously by collectors, art critics, and museum curators. The digital art market may be in its infancy, but if IRIS Graphics can list over 25 internationally known museums in their ads that have added or are exhibiting IRIS prints in their collections, you can be sure the art business is changing. A range of opportunities exists for everyone who is interested in creating, exhibiting, and selling digitally-based art.

Bibliography

This list contains only some of the writings that were useful in the making of this book. This bibliography is by no means a complete record of all the works and sources we have consulted. It indicates the substance and range of reading upon which we have formed our ideas; we intend it to serve as a convenience for those who wish to pursue the study of art.

Dawley, Joseph and Gloria. *Seeing and Painting the Colors of Nature*. New York, NY: Watson-Guptill, 1987.

Haynes, Barry; Crumpler, Wendy. *Photoshop 4 Artistry*. Indianapolis, IN: New Riders Publishing, 1997.

Huntly, Moira. *Painting & Drawing Boats*. Cincinnati, OH: Northlight Books, 1985.

Miller, David; Martin, Diana. *Getting Started in Airbrush*. Cincinnati, OH: Northlight Books, 1993.

Ocvirk, Otto G; Bone, Robert O.; Stinson, Robert E.; Wigg, Philip R. *Art Fundamentals Theory and Practice*. 3rd ed. Dubuque, IA: Wm. C. Brown Company, 1975.

Owen, Peter; Sutcliffe, John. *The Complete Airbrush and Photo-Retouching Manual*. Cincinnati, OH: Northlight Books, 1985.

Pumphrey, Richard. *Elements of Art*. Upper Saddle River, NJ: Prentice Hall, 1996.

Simpson, Ian. *The Encyclopedia of Drawing Techniques*. Seacaucus, NJ: Quarto Publishing plc, 1987.

Webb, Frank. *Strengthen Your Paintings with Dynamic Composition*. Cincinnati, OH: Northlight Books, 1994.

Glossary Art terms used in this book

Abstract Expressionism

A form of artistic representation that stylizes, rearranges, or simplifies what the artist sees.

Additive Process

The building up, modeling, or assembly of a medium.

Adjacent Colors

Colors next to each other on the color wheel or spectrum.

Atmosphere

A combination of the individual elements of weather, buildings, trees, or people together with a state of mind to create a mood.

Balance

The deliberate arrangement of visual elements to imply equilibrium.

Blending

A gradual transition from light to dark or from one color to another.

Complementary Colors

Colors that are opposite one another on the color wheel.

Composition

Arrangement of elements in such a way as to create a harmonious whole.

Contrast

Differences that are evident through comparison.

Cool Colors

Any colors containing blue, such as green, violet, or blue green, which are associated with water, sky, or air.

Crosshatch

A form of shading that combines two or more sets of parallel lines, one set crossing the other at an angle.

Dot

The smallest visual component on a two-dimensional ground, having enough contrast against the ground to be visible.

Emotional Content

Mood created in an artistic work through use of color or other techniques.

Expression

The special characteristics of form that mark the work of an artist or group of artists.

Figure/Ground Relationship

The relationship of subject matter against background on the picture plane.

Freehand

Lines drawn without mechanical assistance such as a ruler or compass.

Grid

A series of evenly spaced rules placed on a drawing surface to guide the placement of objects.

Ground

Any physical material on which a two-dimensional image is created.

Hue

The common name of a color, indicating its position in the color spectrum. Hue is determined by the specific wavelength of the color in the ray of light.

Impressionism

An artistic form of expression emphasizing form rather than subject matter. A nineteenth-century movement that represented special conditions of light and atmosphere, characterized by such painters as Auguste Renoir and Claude Monet.

Lighting

Illumination cast on subject matter by a light source.

Line

The mark made by a tool or instrument as it is drawn across a surface.

Naturalism

Objective recording of observed subject matter.

Negative shape

The unoccupied or empty space left after shapes have been laid down by the artist.

Orthographic

Projection of a single view (such as the front) in an architectural drawing of an object as if all surfaces were in the same plane.

Perspective

The technique or process of representing on a plane or curved surface the spatial relation of objects as they might appear to the eye.

Picture Plane

An implied surface area spanning all of the points on the interior of the picture frame.

Pigment

Coloring matter or substances that the artist uses to create the effect of color on a surface.

Point of View

A position from which something is considered or evaluated.

Realism

A style of art that relies on a high degree of accuracy in representing the appearance of objects.

Receding Space

An area of a picture that appears to recede away from or behind the area of the picture plane.

Reflectivity

Illumination bounced onto a form from a surface; a secondary light source providing indirect light.

Scratchboard

Also called Scraperboard; a soft board that has been coated with a color and that can be easily marked with a sharp instrument to reveal a different color underneath..

Shadow

The dark area of a form that does not receive direct illumination, usually because it is blocked by another form.

Shape

A two- or three-dimensional area with an implied or actual limit.

Silhouette

The area that exists between or is bounded by the edges of an object.

Simultaneous Contrast

The direct contact between two colors that tends to reduce the similarities and intensify the differences.

Subtractive Process

In traditional mediums, refers to the removal of stone or wood in sculpture. In the digital medium, the removal of layers or pixels.

Surrealism

A nineteenth- and twentieth-century art movement that uses dreamlike, fanciful images which appear to come from the subconscious.

Texture

The actual or implied tactile quality of a surface. An actual texture stimulates a tactile response when touched. An implied texture is created by copying the light and dark patterns characteristic of a surface.

Tonality

A careful selection and arrangement of colors, taking into consideration hue, value, and intensity.

Transparency

A quality in paint that enables it to be seen through to partially reveal the background or other layers of paint below.

Value

The tonal quality of lightness or darkness of a surface determined by the amount of light reflected from it.

Volume

The space occupied by an object.

Warm Colors

Red, orange, and yellow colors, which are associated with the sun or fire.

Wash

A lightly applied, semi-transparent coating of color that allows lines, shapes, or other colors to show through.

Appendix A Digital fine art output resources

In this appendix you'll find a wide range of resources to guide your decisions in outputting your fine art. These include a list of wide-format digital printing equipment and supplies, vendors, companies who offer fine art digital printing services, and information about the International Association of Fine Art Digital Printmakers (IAFADP).

Wide-format color printing vendors

Following is a list of some of the companies that manufacture wide-format color printers and/or ink and media for those systems. Don't forget to regularly check the web sites of these companies for the latest updates on equipment, ink, and media development. Although these equipment manufacturers might not guarantee the results, many artists find traditional printmaking papers are a better media option. More information about ink and media is under the section below, "Ink and Media."

American Ink Jet

13 Alexander Rd.
Billerica, MA 01821
Phone: (800) 33AMJET
Fax: (508) 670-5637
http://www.amjet.com

CalComp Technology, Inc.

2411 West La Palma Avenue
Anaheim, CA 92801-2689
Phone: (714) 821-2000
Fax: (714) 821-2832
http://www.calcomp.com/

ColorSpan Corporation
(formerly LaserMaster)

6900 Shady Oak Road
Eden Prairie, MN 55344
Customer Service:
(800) 925-0563
http://www.colorspan.com/

Cymbolic Sciences

P.O. Box 4147
Blaine, WA 98231-4147
Phone: (360) 332-4054
Fax: (360) 332-8032
http://www.cymbolic.com

EPSON America, Inc.

20770 Madrona Avenue
D1-04A
Torrance, CA 90509-2843
Technical Phone Support:
US & Canada (800) 922-8911
Accessories (800) 873-7766
Fax Advice (800) 442-2110
http://www.epson.com/

ENCAD

6059 Cornerstone Court W.
San Diego, CA 92121
Phone: (619) 452-0882
Technical Support Fax:
(619) 546-0659
http://www.encad.com/

Hewlett-Packard Company

Customer Information Center
6:00 AM to 5:00 PM PST
Phone: (800) 752-0900
http://www.hp.com/

ILFORD PHOTO
(USA & Latin America)

West 70 Century Road
Paramus, NJ 07653
Phone: (201) 265-6000
http://www.ilford.com/

IRIS Graphics

Six Crosby Drive
Bedford, MA 01730
Phone: (617) 275-8777
Fax: (617) 275-8590
http://www.irisgraphics.com/

Kodak

Digital Imaging Support
Center
9 am - 8 pm Mon-Fri EDT
In USA: 800-235-6325
Outside USA:
1-716-726-7260
http://www.kodak.com/

Mimaki

http://www.mimaki.co.jp/

Xerox Corporation

Office Document Products
Group
200 Canal View Boulevard
Rochester, NY 14623
Phone: 716-427-4375
http://www.xerox.com/

Fine art digital printmakers

The following are some of the companies that offer services for printing limited editions of art works created in either new or traditional media:

AKA Color

Torrance, CA 90501
Phone: (310) 787-2045

Art Works

Pasadena, CA
Phone: (818) 449-3840

August Editions

San Luis Obispo, CA
Phone: (805) 781-3150

Bishop Street Press

Kihei, HI
Phone: (808) 874-8808

Claes Photo Lab

Antwerp, Belgium
Phone: (323) 541-1636

Classic Editions

Costa Mesa, CA
Phone: (714) 432-7212

Cone Editions

East Topsham, VT
Phone: (802) 439-5751

CrossTech Communications

Chicago, IL
Phone: (312) 787-8200

David Adamson Editions

Washington, DC
Phone: (202) 347-0090

Delta Marketing Group, Inc.

Paradise Valley, AZ
Phone: (602) 998-8280

Electric Images

Minneapolis, MN
Phone: (612) 340-9536

Electric Paintbrush

Milford, MA
Phone: (508) 435-7726

Electronic Imaging Center

Boston, MA
Phone: (617) 292-6226

Evercolor Fine Art

Worcester, MA
Phone: (508) 798-6612

Finer Image Editions

Van Nuys, CA
Phone: (818) 786-8151

The Forethought Group

Batesville, IN
Phone: (812) 934-7424

Gamma One Conversions

New York, NY
Phone: (212) 925-5778

Graphiti Imaging

Saint Clair Shores, MI
Phone: (810) 415-5540

Graphic Trust

Encinitas, CA
Phone: (619) 632-9991

Harvest Productions

Placentia, CA
Phone: (714) 961-1212

Hunter Editions

Kennebunkport, ME
Phone: (207) 967-2802

Imagic

Hollywood, CA
Phone: (213) 461-7766

Interwest Graphics

Salt Lake City, UT
Phone: (801) 973-6720

Jonathan Singer Imaging

Boston, MA
Phone: (617) 423-3484

Kells Editions

San Jose, CA
Phone: (408) 292-4445

Litho-Krome Company

Columbus, CA
Phone: (706) 660-6609

Luminus Editions

New York, NY
Phone: (212) 736-1427

Millstone Editions

Arlington, MA
Phone: (617) 641-3344

Michael M. Coleman & Assoc.

Provo, UT
Phone: (801) 373-9177

Muse [X] Imaging

Los Angeles, CA
Phone: (213) 850-3000

Nash Editions

Manhattan Beach, CA
Phone: (310) 545-4352

Nomi Wagner Photographics

Santa Monica, CA
Phone: (310) 319-1957

Old Town Editions, Inc.

Alexandria, VA
Phone: (703) 684-0005

Salon IRIS

Vienna, Austria
Phone: 43-1/522-72-92

Stella Color

Seattle, WA
Phone: (206) 286-8265

Sutton Graphics

Toronto, Canada
Phone: (416) 598-4031

Skylark Images

Santa Rosa, CA
Phone: (707) 569-7593

Thundercloud Studio

Berkeley, CA
Phone: (510) 848-2941

Thunderbird Editions

Clearwater, FL
Phone: (813) 449-0949

True Colours Reproductions

N. Vancouver, Canada
Phone: (604) 984-7377

Trade associations

To establish a common standard of excellence, some fine art digital printmaking pioneers decided to form a trade association in 1997, The International Association of Fine Art Digital Printmakers (IAFADP). The following statement is from the association's web site membership information page:

The objectives of the IAFADP are to encourage and support the development of the fine art digital printmaking industry. The group will develop standards, definitions and practices intended to promote the orderly integration of developing digital technology into the fine art industry. The functions of the group will be to educate the industry while driving research on issues such as the stability of digital prints. The Association will also share information on new technologies, color management methods and methods to enhance the quality of printmaking. Fine Art Digital Printmakers use different supports and techniques to create original works of fine art in limited edition prints, working in collaboration with and according to the wishes of the artist. The original contemporary print is generally signed and numbered. The authenticity of the signature, the integrity of the numbering and the veracity of the documentation are the responsibility of the printer, publisher and the artist. The International Association of Fine Art Digital Printmakers will uphold the highest standards in printing collaborations between artist and printmaker and work conscientiously to advance the state of the art in digital printmaking.

For more information contact:

The International Association of Fine Art Digital Printmakers

233 N. Market Street, Suite 285
San Jose, CA 95110
Phone: (408) 286-3000 or toll free (888) 239-9099
Fax: (408) 292-4447 *http://www.iafadp.org*

Appendix B Ink and media

This appendix presents test results from studies conducted by Wilhelm Imaging Research to predict display-life of specific ink and paper combinations, and a counter-point discussion of the IRIS printer ink sets controversy by Mac Holbert, cofounder and operations manager for Nash Editions. It concludes with tips for handling and caring for works of art and a list of resource publications.

Life of Displayed Inkjet and Photographic Prints (Uncoated)

Distributed at the 1997 meeting in San Francisco of the International Association of Fine Art Digital Printmakers

©1997 by Wilhelm Imaging Research, Inc.
713 State Street, Grinnell, Iowa 50112 U.S.A.
Tel: 515-236-4284 • Fax: 515-236-4222
E-mail: hwilhelm@aol.com

Iris Graphics Equipoise Ink Set

Arches Cold Press	(tests in progress)
Somerset Velvet Paper	20–24 years
Iris Canvas	16–18 years
Arches for Iris Paper	13–15 years
Liege Inkjet Fine Art Paper	2–3 years

Lyson Fine Arts Ink Set (FA-II M; ID C; FA-I Y+B)

Arches Cold Press	(tests in progress)
Somerset Velvet Paper	20–24 years
Iris Canvas	(tests in progress)
Arches for Iris Paper	(tests in progress)
Liege Inkjet Fine Art Paper	2–3 years

ConeTech Wide Gamut Fine Art Ink Set

Arches Cold Press Paper	(tests in preparation)
Somerset Velvet Paper	20–24 years
Arches for Iris	(tests in preparation)
Iris Canvas	(tests in preparation)

American Ink Jet Corp. "NE" Inks (C+M; Lyson FA-I Y+B)

Somerset Velvet Paper	4–6 years

ENCAD GO Ink Set (pigment-based inks)

ENCAD Photo Glossy Paper	>50 years
ENCAD Canvas	>50 years

ENCAD GA Ink Set (dye-based inks)

ENCAD Photo Glossy Paper	
ENCAD Canvas	1–2 years

ENCAD GS Ink Set (dye-based inks)

ENCAD Photo Glossy Paper	1–2 years

Ilford Archiva Inks for ENCAD Printers (dye-based inks)

Ilford Ilfojet Photo Glossy Paper	>40 years

Epson Stylus 3000 17x22-inch Printer (standard Epson inks)

Fuji Super Photo Grade Inkjet Paper	4–5 years
Epson Photo Quality Glossy White Film	2–3 years
Epson Photo Quality Glossy Paper	2 years
Epson Photo Quality Ink Jet Paper (matte)	1–2 years
Kodak Photo Weight Premium Glossy Paper	6 months

Current Photographic Color Negative Prints

Fujicolor Super FA Paper Type 5	71 years
Kodak Ektacolor Edge 5 Paper	16 years
Konica Color QA Paper Type A6	14 years
Agfacolor Paper Type 10	13 years

Ilford Ilfochrome Silver Dye-Bleach Photographic Prints

Ilford Ilfochrome Classic Deluxe polyester–base	29 years★
Ilford Ilfochrome RC-base prints	29 years★

*tentative data based on tests completed in 1992 with Ilford Cibachrome II polyester-base and RC-base print materials

What's up with the IRIS ink sets?

by Mac Holbert, cofounder and operations manager for Nash Editions, a California fine arts digital printmaker who helped pioneer IRIS Giclée printing.

Lately controversy has surrounded the various ink sets available for the IRIS inkjet printer. Henry Wilhelm, a world authority on ink permanence, recently released results regarding several of the most widely used ink sets for displayed ink jet prints to the International Association of Fine Art Digital Printmakers. Although Mr. Wilhelm provides an invaluable service to the printing and printmaking industry, his published results *do not* take into consideration the color space of the ink set being tested.

Theoretically, one could submit four bottles of the most permanent ink component available (four bottles of Lyson High Intensity Fine Art Black, for example) and label them Cyan, Magenta, Yellow, and Black. The permanence test would be spectacular, but printing an image with this ink set would be disastrous on an aesthetic level. Nash Editions finds the magenta component of all of the so-called "permanent" ink sets to be lacking. They can be marginally useful when printing on coated surfaces, but on untreated fine art watercolor papers, they reproduce red as a brickish-red, more orange than red.

An IRIS print must not be judged on permanence alone. Art is not about permanence; art is about aesthetics and vision. Is a watercolor less of an artistic expression because it is more fugitive than an oil painting, or is a C-print less meaningful because it is less permanent than an IlfaChrome? Artists rarely pause to consider permanence when inspiration strikes. Photographer and painter David Hockney commented specifically on the permanence of IRIS prints by simply stating that "colour is fugitive in life, like it is in pictures. Indeed colour is the most fugitive element in all pictures, a great deal more than line. Dimming the light alters color. It does not alter line." When, and if, an ink set is developed that is more permanent *and* can more accurately translate one's vision to paper, Nash Editions will be the first to adopt it.

Tips for Handling and Caring for Works of Art

The Odyssey Group, which publishes magazines on collecting autographs, poster art and other memorabilia, offers tips for handling works of art on paper at the following web site: *http://www.odysseygroup.com/acm297/sidebar.htm.*

In addition to discussing how you physically handle, display, and store works on paper, an article titled *Preserving Manuscripts and Documents* by F.Colin Kingston offers a brief list of publications and organizations that offer in-depth tips on document preservation and can be found at *http://www.odysseygroup.com/acm297/preserve.htm.*

Another resource is the web site of WAAC, the Western Association for Art Conservation at *http://palimpsest.stanford.edu/waac/.*

The following article posted at the WAAC web site offers an excellent insight into the problems faced by museums and galleries in handling fragile works of art. We recommend checking it out. Its URL: *http://palimpsest.stanford.edu/waac/wn/wn07/wn07-2/wn07-203.html.*

WAAC Newsletter

Volume 7, Number 2, May 1985, pp. 3-11
Handling Large Works of Art on Paper: 6 Interviews

Interviews conducted by: Linda Shaffer, Paper Conservator
Interviews with:

Sidney Felson, Co-Owner, Gemini G.E.L., Los Angeles
Peter Goulds, Gallery Owner and Director, L.A. Louver
Gallery, Venice, California
Denise Domergue, President, Conservation of Paintings, Ltd.,
Los Angeles
Paula Kendall, Print Department, Sotheby Parke Bernet, Los
Angeles
Victoria Blyth Hill, Senior Paper Conservator, Los Angeles
County Museum of Art, Los Angeles
Sam Francis, Artist, Los Angeles, Tokyo, Paris, Bern

Other Helpful Publications

Hands on Paper

The Technical Supplement to *On Paper–The Journal of Prints, Drawing and Photography*

39 East 78th Street
New York, NY 10021
Phone: (212) 988-5959
Contact: Bill Jones, Editor
E-mail: info@onpaper.com

Art Business News

A publication addressing the business aspect of art and framing. Editorial covers everything from trends and sales to new colors and the latest tax changes. Published monthly. An ADVANSTAR PUBLICATION.

For information contact:

Michelle Mitchell, Advanstar Communications
1-800-225-4569
E-mail: *Information@advanstar.com*
Subscriptions: *http://www.superfill.com/subscribe/abn.htm*
Phone: (800) 346-0085 ext. 477

Index

P